Under the Power Lines

A Bible Study in the Power of God

By Diana Endicott
©2016

UNDER THE POWER LINES
A Bible Study in the Power of God
by Diana Endicott ©2016

Illustrated by Jessica Broich

See more of her artwork here: http://www.artisticembers.com

Cover photo used with permission: iStock.com/Getty Images.

All Bible references are from the New American Standard Bible unless otherwise noted.
Scripture quotations taken from the New American Standard Bible® (NASB),
Copyright © 1960, 1962, 1963, 1968, 1971, 1972, 1973,
1975, 1977, 1995 by The Lockman Foundation
Used by permission. www.Lockman.org

The Message
"Scriptures taken from The Message. Copyright © 1993, 1994, 1995, 1996, 2000, 2001,
2002. Used by permission of NavPress Publishing Group."

New International Version (NIV)
"THE HOLY BIBLE, NEW INTERNATIONAL VERSION®, NIV® Copyright © 1973,
1978, 1984, 2011 by Biblica, Inc.® Used by permission. All rights reserved worldwide."

English Standard Version (ESV)
The Holy Bible, English Standard Version® (ESV®), Copyright © 2001 by Crossway, a
publishing ministry of Good News Publishers. All rights reserved. ESV Text Edition: 2011

NET Version (note: they prefer these initials rather than spelled out)
Scripture quoted by permission. All scripture quotations, unless otherwise indicated, are
taken from the NET Bible® copyright ©1996-2016 by Biblical Studies Press, L.L.C. All
rights reserved."

Modern English Version:
"Scripture taken from the Modern English Version. Copyright © 2014 by Military Bible
Association. Used by permission. All rights reserved."

No part of this book may be reproduced or transmitted in any form or by any means,
electronic or mechanical, including photocopying or recording, or by any information storage
or retrieval system, except as may be expressly permitted in writing by author. Requests for
permission should be addressed to Diana Endicott at endicottdiana@yahoo.com

Lessons

Chapter One: The Power to be Loved and to Love

Chapter Two: The Power to be Strong

Chapter Three: The Power to be Held Together

Chapter Four: The Power for a Changed Heart

Chapter Five: The Power to See with Spiritual Eyes

Chapter Six: The Power to Hope and Bring Hope

Chapter Seven: The Power to be Present in His Presence

Chapter Eight: The Power to Walk in Agreement

Chapter Nine: The Power to Walk with Purpose

Chapter Ten: The Power to be Powerful

Introduction

On June 15th, 2009 I went for a walk in our five-acre woods and began to pray my personal agreement with Hosea 6:3: "I will acknowledge you, Lord, I will press on to acknowledge You. For as surely as the sun rises, You will appear. You will come to us like the winter rains, like the spring rains that water the earth."

As I prayed and got to the end of our property, I came into a large area that had been cleared for the power lines behind us. The clearing had large towers with a view into the valley, both northeast and southwest. As I stood there admiring the view, I believe I heard God say something to me.

By "heard God," I mean I had a clear thought that I've learned to recognize as not my own. God speaks to us in many different ways and we can learn to hear His voice (see John 10:27).

I heard, "Meet Me here every day and I will teach you about My power." I stood and pondered this for a moment, as it's always wise to check to make sure it's God we're hearing and not the influence of the pizza we had the night before. I concluded that there is no way I would make this up, and God subsequently brought many confirmations.

And so began a journey of 101 visits under the power lines - a time of deeper listening and pondering together, which has led to more study. As with all journeys, there were unfortunate detours, distractions and delays, but also deeper moments, discoveries and decisions. Over time it became clear that this time under the power lines was not just for me, and so this Bible study began to take shape. I'm looking forward to all God will do with His scriptures and insights that He will give us as we journey together in this study about His power, walking together "Under the Power Lines".

A prayer as we begin

Father, we want to hear what You have to say, and learn what You want to teach us. We choose to have open hearts and discerning minds. Thank you for being our Teacher, Holy Spirit. Help us to follow as You guide us. Amen.

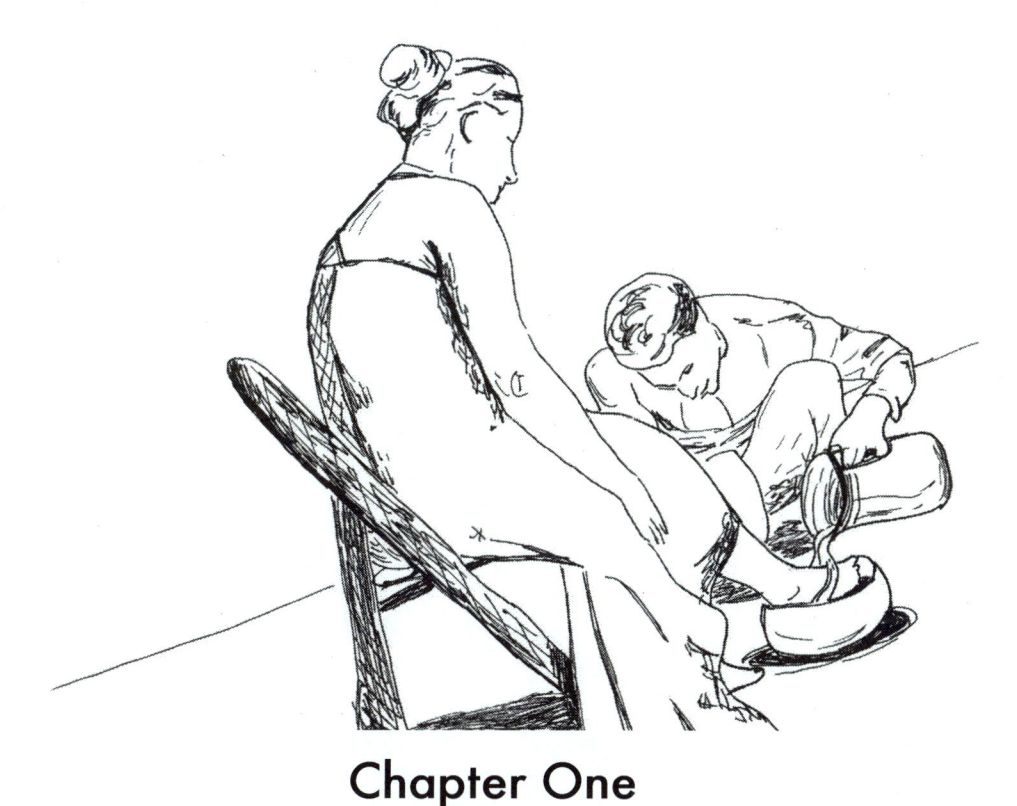

Chapter One

The Power to be Loved and to Love

On the first day under the power lines I stood listening and waiting. I saw the lines and towers more clearly. I sensed God saying that both the lines and towers were symbolic - representing people. The towers symbolically represented strategically-placed leaders to help keep the lines off the ground, out of danger and functioning properly. The lines symbolically represented people held carefully in the best possible way and function so that power will flow through them. God was helping me understand that His power flows through His people to bring light, help and resource to others.

On day 13 under the power lines I heard, "Power in a human life whose source is self leads to ruin eventually (relational, spiritual, even physical); but My power in a human life brings abundant life and light and joy and meaning in dark places. Everywhere you go you bring the potential of transformation to a person or place... *It's always about people* - My heart always beats for people. My power comes from the core of Who I am - loving, kind, faithful, all-wise, all-knowing."

Many times He emphasized that it's all about people. This makes sense, of course, because God is always focused on His beloved - the people He created and so deeply loves.

On day 20 under the power lines I heard, "My power is never for selfish display or extravagant demonstration for its own sake. It isn't intended to impress the flesh but to free the spirit of man, whom I love. My purposes guide the flow of My power." So, to understand God's power, we need to begin our study by understanding His purposes - His passion for people and His love and desire to be in relationship with them. **God's power is never a detached display of fierce force, but rather an intentional energy that draws us toward Himself. His powerful love reaches to us to draw us to Himself.**

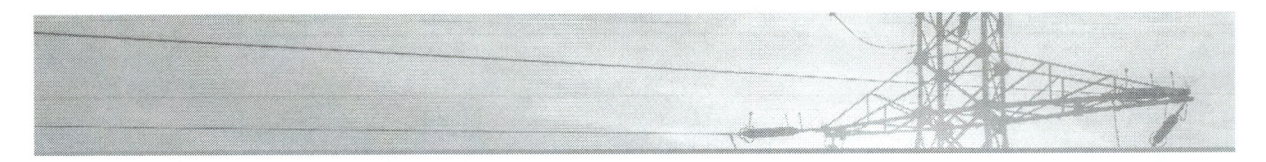

The Power to Be Loved

In the Old Testament one of the words for "love" is *ahabah*, which is used over 40 times to depict the love of God as well as human love. It's interesting that it's first used in Genesis to describe what Jacob felt for Rachel: Genesis 29:20: "So Jacob served seven years for Rachel and they seemed to him but a few days because of his love (*ahabah*) for her."

The first time *ahabah* is used for God's love is in Deuteronomy 7:8: "But because the LORD loved (*ahabah*) you and kept the oath which He swore to your forefathers, the LORD brought you out by a mighty hand, and redeemed you from the house of slavery, from the hand of Pharaoh king of Egypt."

Other places where *ahabah* is used for God's love include the following. Note what you see in these verses about His love:

Song of Solomon 2:4

_____

Jeremiah 31:3

_____

Zephaniah 3:17

_____

Perhaps you've noticed in these verses that God's love always seems to involve some sort of action: He brings us to a place, He draws us, He sings and rejoices over us. It always has movement, purposeful movement.

Understanding this helps us understand the New Testament word for God's love: *Agapao* or *agape*. Perhaps the most famous verse that reveals God's kind of love, this *agapao*, is found in John 3:16: "For God so loved (*agapao*) the world, that He gave His only begotten Son, that whoever believes in Him shall not perish but have eternal life." **God's love always involves action of some sort focused on the well-being and welfare of the one that is loved.** The word "world" in John 3:16 is not defining the planet or globe, but rather its occupants - us! We are the beloved of God, so loved that He took action for our well-being

-6-

and welfare for all eternity. He sent Jesus, His only Son, truly Himself in human form, to redeem our brokenness to a restored relationship with Him. He took our sins upon Himself and gives His righteousness to those who receive Him. For some of us reading this today, we are remembering the time we chose to receive this redemption and restoration through Jesus Christ. I hope you are savoring the beauty of your salvation anew.

For some of us this may be a new thought to consider. My deepest hope is that as you consider God's love for you, revealed in His actions through Jesus Christ, you will come to a decision to accept this great love expressed through Jesus. It's as simple as a prayerful "yes" to God and a surrender to His *agapao* love. Perhaps there was a time you had said "yes" to God but have drifted away in distraction or dismay. His *agapao* love is always active to draw us back to Himself, working even now as you read this. He will always be focused on your well-being and welfare, whether you see it or not; always working to bring you to wholeness in your relationship with Him; always intentionally using His resources to draw us closer.

This would be a good time to **selah** (a Hebrew word found in scripture meaning to "pause and think about that").

It's one thing to accept that God loves people - after all, one might say that's His job, so to speak. It's quite another thing to experience the love of God yourself, to seek and then find Him - because His power is always working to draw us to Himself.

I like this quote from Graham Cooke, a very helpful Bible teacher: "Every day we start afresh in God's love. We carry over no negative into the next dawn. When the sun rises fresh to greet the day, so do we. It suits the enemy for us never to discover freshness as a way of life. Because he has no access to God's abundance, the devil is weary. All he can do is try to make everyone as he is - burdened, angry, resentful, and bitter. We live in daylight compartments. We live, one day at a time. The mindset with which you begin each day will support your next experience of either God or the enemy." (from *Secret Sayings, Hidden Meanings*)

Every morning brings an opportunity for us, a choice to receive and walk in His love or not. It can be a simple choice as you wake up each morning, or perhaps more of an "experience" that makes an impression to help you remember.

I remember a time when I was standing in a little room just off the makeshift pharmacy of our short-term medical/dental missions setup in a small school in Palencia, Guatemala. My interpreter and I had just finished a time of sharing the gospel with those who were waiting for their medications, and were wanting to hear the gospel story told through colorful bracelets. Everyone had left, and I think we were getting ready to head over to our lunch area when a woman came running up to us, crying hard and saying something in Spanish I couldn't understand. Even my interpreter couldn't quite understand her because she was crying so hard. She kept pointing to her heart, so I had a quick thought that we needed to get Dr. Tito, our

Guatemalan medical leader, to see her pronto. Maybe she was having a heart attack! But after a tense moment or two of our undivided attention, my interpreter was able to finally understand her and turned to me to say, "She wants to receive Jesus into her heart!" I tried to hide my surprise as I had not yet had anyone run up to me in the United States crying and begging to receive Jesus Christ; but as I turned to look into her teary eyes and nodded my head, she fell to her knees. We joined her and huddled together in a holy embrace as she prayed a sincere prayer of gratitude for Jesus coming in love and power to cleanse her soul and give her a new life. Afterwards she stood up smiling and crying, shaking our hands, pointing to her grateful heart once again, thanking us. I'll never forget being a witness of the love of God experienced in a sore heart ready to receive Him.

How's your heart today? Even if you already have a personal relationship and experience with God, it's possible there are days when the need for a fresh encounter makes us feel like running to the next available willing servant to fall to our knees together to experience Him and His powerful, holy embrace. It may be, however, that even with a tremendous longing, you have not had an experience or encounter of this dramatic impact. You may wonder if there is something wrong or if He simply "embraces" other people. Let me assure you that He is with you and you can continue on in the very real embrace of God, whether you feel it or not. With me, sometimes it is simply a choice to believe, an act of my will, whether I have a dramatic encounter or not.

Jesus tells us in John 15:9, "Just as the Father has loved Me, I have also loved you; abide in My love." Some translations say "dwell" or "continue" in my love; meaning to remain, not depart, be held - a holy embrace indeed. I must choose to believe in His love, but then I must also choose to remain in it. This may take some effort or action.

I'm recommending that you take some action now. Some places in the New Testament where "*agapao*" is used are listed below. **Personalize these verses and read them out loud (shut the door, no one will mind).** Put your name where you see the words "we" or "us" or "you" or "your". You can use your given name also - whatever helps your soul hear the beauty and truth of the love of God in these verses.

To take this a step further, make it a personal conversation with God, and hopefully a personal experience, by replacing the word/name "God" or "Father", or "Jesus" with "you". An example: Romans 5:8 - "But YOU showed YOUR love for ME in that while I was still a sinner, YOU died for ME." When we personalize scripture, we are receiving it - sometimes deep into our soul. This may take some extra effort, but I believe it will be worth it.

Ephesians 2:4-5: "But God, being rich in mercy, because of His LOVE with which He loved us, even when we were dead in our transgressions, made us alive together with Christ - by grace you have been saved."

Galatians 2:20: "I have been crucified with Christ, and it is no longer I who live, but Christ lives in me; and the life which I now live in the flesh I live by faith in the Son of God, who loved me and gave Himself up for me."

Zephaniah 3:17 (The Message): "...Don't despair. Your God is present among you, a strong Warrior there to save you. Happy to have you back, He'll calm you with His love and delight you with His songs."

1 Peter 5:6-7: "Therefore humble yourselves under the mighty hand of God, that He may exalt you at the proper time, casting all your anxiety on Him, because He cares for you."

I John 4:9-10 (NIV): "This is how God showed His love among us: He sent his one and only Son into the world that we might live through Him. This is love: not that we loved God, but that He loved us and sent His Son as an atoning sacrifice for our sins."

Romans 8:37-39: "But in all these things we overwhelmingly conqueror through Him who loved us. For I am convinced that neither death nor life, nor angels nor principalities, nor things present nor things to come, nor powers, nor height, nor depth, nor any other created thing, will be able to separate us from the love of God which is in Christ Jesus our Lord."

Sometimes writing out our thoughts is helpful to clarify, even solidify them. Jot down other verses about God's love that come to mind and journal any thoughts about this exercise here:

_____

_____

_____

_____

_____

I hope the truth of His *agapao* love is taking you deeper in your understanding of just how much He loves you, right now, right where you are. I hope you are able to truly know His great love for you not just as some theological truth but as a personal experience, whether it's felt in a dramatic way or not. **It's with this foundational belief and understanding of God's intentionality and focus on our well-being that will help us set the stage for His power to continue to flow in and through us.**

The Power to Love

Experiencing God's love brings a stable foundation for His power to flow into my life. But it doesn't stop there. On the second day under the power lines I heard, "(Electrical) power is dangerous and needs care and 'protocol'. If large regional towers go down, the whole region is affected, but it is very hard to take a tower down. It would take a catastrophe." This early caution helped me to see that we are not isolated islands all by ourselves. Just as these regional power lines carefully allow the electrical current to go where it needs to go, our lives affect others in sometimes profound ways, whether we see it or not.

We've seen that God's power is the intentional effort that always draws us to Himself. Now we'll see that He chooses to use ordinary people like you and me to be the expression of His love, His drawing power, on earth.

It is an important Kingdom principle that as we receive the *agapao* love of God, it changes our hearts so that we can *agapao* love others. When I receive His Spirit, I am receiving all of Him, including what He carries in His heart for us and for others. And so it is that God can ask that we love as He loves. Circle the word "love" in the following verses (this will help us see that He is serious about this):

1 John 4: 7-8
"Beloved, let us love one another, for love is from God, and everyone who loves is born of God and knows God. The one who does not love does not know God, for God is love."

John 13:34-35 (NIV)
"A new command I give to you: love one another. As I have loved you, so you must love one another. By this everyone will know that you are my disciples, if you love one another."

I Corinthians 13:1-13 (ESV)
"If I speak in the tongues of men and of angels, but have not love, I am a noisy gong or a clanging cymbal. And if I have prophetic powers, and understand all mysteries and all knowledge, and if I have all faith, so as to remove mountains, but have not love, I am nothing. If I give away all I have, and if I deliver up my body to be burned, but have not love, I gain nothing. Love is patient and kind; love does not envy or boast; it is not arrogant or rude. It does not insist on its own way; it is not irritable or resentful; it does not rejoice at wrongdoing, but rejoices with the truth. Love bears all things, believes all things, hopes all things, endures all things. Love never ends. As for prophecies, they will pass away; as for tongues, they will cease; as for knowledge, it will pass away. For we know in part and we prophesy in part, but when the perfect comes, the partial will pass away. When I was a child, I spoke like a child, I thought like a child, I reasoned like a child. When I became a man, I gave up childish ways. For now we see in a mirror dimly, but then face to face. Now I know in part; then I shall know fully, even as I have been fully known. So now faith, hope, and love abide, these three; but the greatest of these is love."

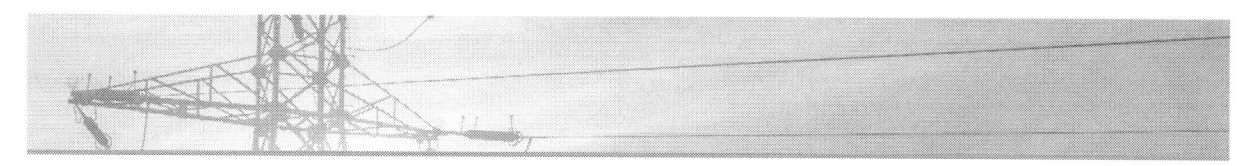

We are in danger of being just a lot of noise without love. I've been "noisy" at times in the past. How about you? **The process of allowing His transforming power in my own heart is the beginning of truly loving as He loves.**

We're not necessarily talking about feelings here. It begins with how we think. Look at Romans 12:1-2 (NIV): "Therefore I urge you, brothers and sisters, in view of God's mercy, to offer your bodies as a living sacrifice, holy and pleasing to God - this is your true and proper worship. Do not conform to the pattern of this world, but be transformed by the renewing of your mind. Then you will be able to test and approve what God's will is - His good, pleasing and perfect will." God does the transforming, by the power He brings to us through the Holy Spirit to help us think differently. He is very creative in how He brings us His perspective, along with the help we need to love others.

Some years ago I was working as a medical transcriptionist and commuting to the clinic each week to deliver the work. One day I was very upset with someone. As I drove, I was rehearsing all the "good reasons" why I was justified in my frustration and anger with them. This went on for some miles. Then suddenly I had a clear thought out of nowhere that they behaved this way due to pain in their own lives. I was not aware of the specific pain that God was pointing out here, but I knew that this was true. Then somehow God's compassion for them rose up within me. Considering the intensity of my frustration, this is something of a miracle. It was the power of God, the divine energy of God bringing me beyond myself and my own thoughts and feelings, drawing me once again to Himself. He transformed my thoughts and gave me His perspective.

As this compassion for them began to grow, it overcame any rehearsed case I had against them. So instead of rehearsing my reasons for being angry with them, I slowly began to reconsider this way of thinking, and eventually began to pray for them with genuine concern for their well-being. My residence and commute was in the Seattle area at the time, so it took quite some time to arrive at the clinic, and I needed every minute of it to cooperate with this process within my mind and heart; but I'm glad I cooperated, and allowed my thoughts to be transformed.

Rehearsing our "case" against others is a form of bondage to a particular time and event and/or the actions of others. I believe God wants us to live in the powerful freedom of thinking differently, no longer in bondage. He will bring His perspective to us if we're willing, and He will bring the power to transform how we think; but we must cooperate with His power and agree with His intentions, one choice at a time. Then our actions will line up to our transformed thoughts. The power of God came to help me change my thinking, and so my actions changed from rehearsing the negative to praying the positive.

Since God's love always involves movement and action, and we have His love within us through the Holy Spirit, He asks that we take action. We've seen that He can expect this, because when I have received the love of God, this *agapao* "current" begins to change my heart towards others so that I will act towards them as He would - even on the freeway in heavy traffic. Impossible, you say? Not with the intentional strength, the power of God. **When I make the decision to love, God brings the strength and power to take the action necessary. It's a partnership.**

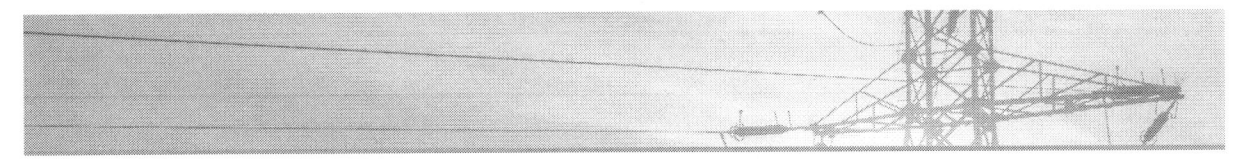

Write down the actions we are instructed to take as we choose to love (*agapao*) others:

Hebrews 13:1-15

_____

_____

Colossians 3:12-15

_____

_____

Luke 6:27-36

_____

_____

I Corinthians 16:14

_____

_____

Well, that last one rather sums it up, doesn't it? Without the power of God, however, we're dangerously vulnerable to being "noisy clanging gongs and cymbals," driving down the freeway clanging away. But God's intentions are that we are the effective, transformed children of God, partnering with Him every day to live power-filled lives of love for others. It starts with an open heart, willing to be transformed.

On day 19 the Lord said to me, "My power is designed to work through connections - from Me to you to others and onward; but the connectors, the touch points, are protected. They are encased in love - My love. With My love/power, there is transformation. If My power is used without love, there is change but it is hazardous. You must be filled with My love for My power to flow. I cannot trust those who do not love selflessly."

Perhaps you have experienced the hazardous outcome of some interactions with a power-hungry person. When we are power-hungry, our motives are varied; but I've noticed it's usually self-preservation at the top of the list, or some sort of self-focused concern. That seems to be one of the disastrous outcomes of our fallen nature without Christ.
But that can change once we choose to entrust our lives to Jesus, who imparts His righteousness to our repentant hearts. As one of God's family members, each of us receives His Spirit to empower us to think as He thinks and love as He loves. Although we are involved in the choice to love, and He is patient with us, you'll notice He does not give us the option as His children not to love.

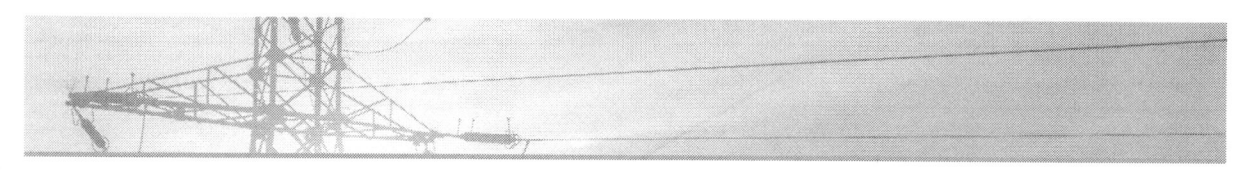

Let's review:

I John 4:7-21: "Beloved, let us **love** one another, for **love** is from God; and everyone who **loves** is born of God and knows God. The one who does not **love** does not know God, for God is **love**. By this the **love** of God was manifested in us, that God has sent His only begotten Son into the world so that we might live through Him. In this is **love**, not that we **loved** God, but that He **loved** us and sent His Son to be the propitiation for our sins. Beloved, if God so **loved** us, we also ought to **love** one another. No one has seen God at any time; if we **love** one another, God abides in us, and His **love** is perfected in us. By this we know that we abide in Him and He in us, because He has given us of His Spirit. We have seen and testify that the Father has sent the Son to be the Savior of the world. Whoever confesses that Jesus is the Son of God, God abides in him, and he in God. We have come to know and have believed the **love** which God has for us. God is **love**, and the one who abides in **love** abides in God, and God abides in him. By this, **love** is perfected with us, so that we may have confidence in the day of judgment; because as He is, so also are we in this world. There is no fear in **love**; but perfect **love** casts out fear, because fear involves punishment, and the one who fears is not perfected in **love**. We **love**, because He first **loved** us. If someone says, "I **love** God," and hates his brother, he is a liar; for the one who does not **love** his brother whom he has seen, cannot **love** God whom he has not seen. And this commandment we have from Him, that the one who **loves** God should **love** his brother also."

How many times did you see the word "love"? _____. I have highlighted the word "love" in bold print, but my prayer is that God is highlighting and igniting His love in your heart, and you are warming up to the idea that He loves you with an everlasting love, and you can love others as He loves others - with His power to do so.

On day 57 under the power lines I heard, "Right relationships are conduits for My love and power to flow. Ask Me for my perspective and once your heart receives it, I'll supply the enabling grace to love and move in My name."

This is a good time to quiet your heart and mind and write down any difficult relationships in one column (use initials if you'd like), and write in the second column what God wants to say to you. Ask Him to show you how to specifically love or forgive or relate or release this person. I understand that some situations are so painful and complicated that it may be wise to simply release it out of your soul into God's mighty hands. That would be an appropriate and powerful prayer of forgiveness.

Biblical forgiveness is a personal decision to release the situation or person from your wounded soul into God's hands. It is a choice that does not require an apology or action from another. It is a holy agreement between you and God, freeing your soul to entrust the person and situation to Him. Reconciliation is another matter altogether, requiring two people to be in agreement. It is time to forgive so your soul can be free, but God must bring about the necessary pieces for reconciliation.

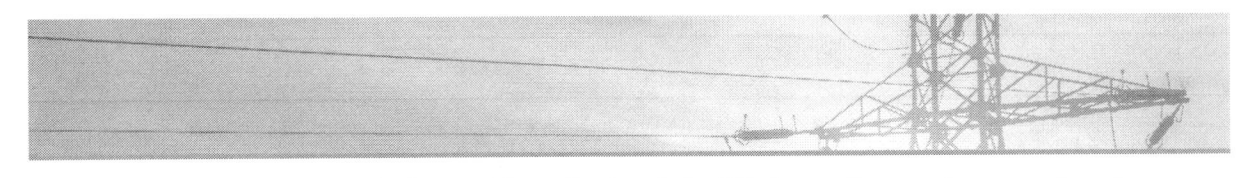

Review the verses above to help you "hear" what is in His heart for you in your situation. (See also https://www.openbible.info/topics/forgiving_each_other). Reach out to someone you trust if you are stuck in this process.

Name	**Action God wants**
_____	_____
_____	_____
_____	_____

If no one came to mind, spend a moment praising God for the beauty of a free heart and soul. But if someone or something did come to mind, pray over your action plan with a trusted friend or counselor.

On day 46 under the power lines I heard: "To understand my power and how it flows, you must understand My love and how it pours from My heart. Receive My love, let Me lavish it upon you - and when it spills over to others, when you love them as I do, My power will flow through you. It will amaze you. It will bless and forever change others around you. It will begin the transformation of entire communities, wherever I send you. Know in your deepest self that I love you...right now...just as you are...always...I mean it."

A suggested prayer as we close

Lord God, I come to You grateful for Your love and boldly declare that I am Yours and You are mine. Even so, I'm aware of my need for Your power to love others. I humbly ask for Your perspective and guidance for loving actions towards others, and I choose now to go as You guide me. Help me to admit when I fail and come to You for renewed energy and power to love again. I repent of my rehearsing the negative, and choose now to see and act with the positive You reveal to me, even if it's as simple as releasing it out of my mind and soul and giving it all to You. In Jesus' name, amen.

Chapter Two

The Power to be Strong

On the third day under the power lines I heard, "Power is made perfect in weakness". The insight came that a line can do nothing by and for itself. It must be moved and worked upon by the hands of experts. The Lord is our expert Linesman! The line is "weak" in that it can do nothing for itself, but power flows through it anyway, appropriately by design. It is appropriate for the line to be in need of an expert Linesman - that is the way it's made. And it is "perfect" when it is functioning in the way it was created to function.

So it is with us! Today we'll see that we are in great need of the dependable work of our Lord, the expert Linesman. We'll also see how His power flows through "weakness".

A suggested prayer as we begin

Today, Lord, I ask for insight and understanding of Your ways. Thank you, Holy Spirit, for being my Teacher and always helping me see Jesus and the ways of the Kingdom. My grateful heart says "amen."

The phrase "power is made perfect in weakness" is found in 2 Corinthians 12:7-9: "To keep me from becoming conceited because of these surpassingly great revelations, there was given me a thorn in my flesh, a messenger of Satan, to torment me. Three times I pleaded with the Lord to take it away from me. But He said to me, 'My grace is sufficient for you, for My power is made perfect in weakness.' Therefore I will boast all the more gladly about my weaknesses, so that Christ's power may rest on me."

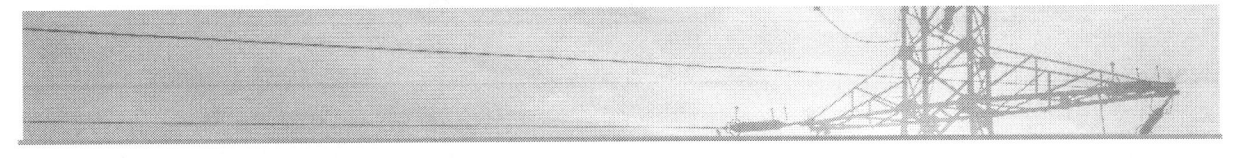

It is so like the Holy Spirit to bring this phrase to my mind under the power lines so that I would remember this verse and we can look it up and reflect on the keys revealed here - keys to understanding and cooperating with God's power. Let's dig into this verse to find the treasures within it.

First, let's set the context. Paul is speaking to the Corinthians, this being his second letter to them. He is making a case regarding his credentials. Let's start at verse 1 of 2 Corinthians 12 (Using ESV translation):

[1] I must go on boasting. Though there is nothing to be gained by it, I will go on to visions and revelations of the Lord. [2] I know a man in Christ who fourteen years ago was caught up to the third heaven—whether in the body or out of the body I do not know, God knows. [3] And I know that this man was caught up into paradise -- whether in the body or out of the body I do not know, God knows - [4] and he heard things that cannot be told, which man may not utter. [5] On behalf of this man I will boast, but on my own behalf I will not boast, except of my weaknesses— [6] though if I should wish to boast, I would not be a fool, for I would be speaking the truth; but I refrain from it, so that no one may think more of me than he sees in me or hears from me. [7] So to keep me from becoming conceited because of the surpassing greatness of the revelations, a thorn was given me in the flesh, a messenger of Satan to harass me, to keep me from becoming conceited. [8] Three times I pleaded with the Lord about this, that it should leave me. [9] But he said to me, "My grace is sufficient for you, for my power is made perfect in weakness." Therefore I will boast all the more gladly of my weaknesses, so that the power of Christ may rest upon me. [10] For the sake of Christ, then, I am content with weaknesses, insults, hardships, persecutions, and calamities. For when I am weak, then I am strong.

Circle the word "boast" or "boasting" in the passage above.

The Greek word for "boast" here is the word *kauchaomai*. It simply means "to glory in a thing, whether with reason or without". We've all met people who boast "without reason". Perhaps, if we're honest, we'll admit that we've boasted in this way too. With this definition in mind, we see that there may be reasons to boast, but it is a dangerous thing. What does Paul say is the reason for the "thorn in his flesh"? (verse 7)

_____

How did Paul know this was the reason?

_____

List what Paul is boasting about (note: the "man" in verse 2 is believed by theologians to be Paul himself, who is using this literary tool to make a point)

In verses 1-4

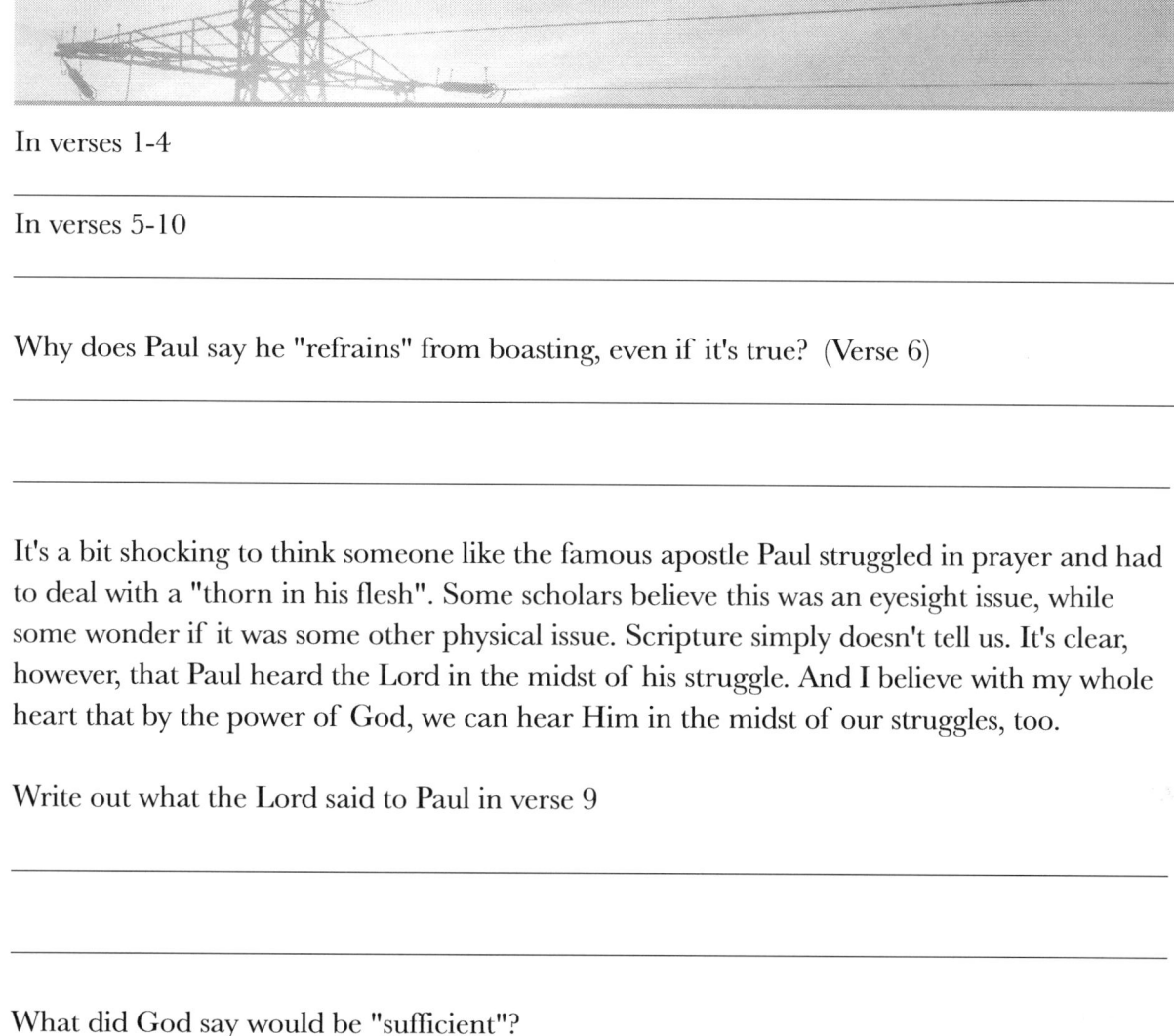

In verses 5-10

Why does Paul say he "refrains" from boasting, even if it's true? (Verse 6)

It's a bit shocking to think someone like the famous apostle Paul struggled in prayer and had to deal with a "thorn in his flesh". Some scholars believe this was an eyesight issue, while some wonder if it was some other physical issue. Scripture simply doesn't tell us. It's clear, however, that Paul heard the Lord in the midst of his struggle. And I believe with my whole heart that by the power of God, we can hear Him in the midst of our struggles, too.

Write out what the Lord said to Paul in verse 9

What did God say would be "sufficient"?

Let's look at this a little more closely. The word "grace" here is the Greek word *charis*. We may have been taught many helpful definitions of God's grace (i.e., unmerited favor, spiritual giftedness, etc.); but *Strong's Concordance* mentions one meaning as "the divine influence upon the heart". The root word of charis is *chairo*, meaning to rejoice, be glad, to rejoice exceedingly, to be well, to thrive! It's a very active word and it sure sounds like some positive influence on a needy heart. I hope this is already good news to you today.

The Greek word for "sufficient" in this passage is *arkeo*, meaning to be possessed of unfailing strength, to be strong, to suffice, to be enough, to defend, ward off, to be satisfied, to be contented. Although a primary word, it is similar to a word meaning "lift up," like a barrier or protection.

So if we put these thoughts and definitions together, perhaps we could translate the first part of what God said to Paul as this: "*My influence upon your heart will bring the strength to ward off anything that makes you discontented, no matter what...*"

Selah.

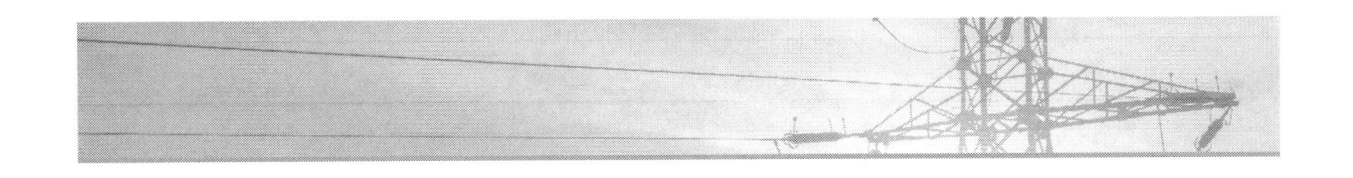

Write the second part of what God said to Paul:

"For _____

The word "for" (Greek word *gar*) assigns a reason for the previous statement. So what is the reason for God's influence upon the heart which brings strength to be satisfied and contented, no matter what? Let's dig a little further....we're almost there.

The word for "power" here is *dynamis*, meaning strength, ability, inherent power, power residing in a thing by virtue of its nature, or which a person or thing exerts and puts forth power for performing miracles, moral power and excellence of soul. It is used 120 times in the New Testament. This should get our attention, and is the main point of this study.

We get our word "dynamite" from this word, and so we may have a mental picture of explosions of some sort. But it seems clear in scripture that the *dynamis* of God can't be understood apart from the character of God - His inherent nature from which He achieves what He purposes by His power. It would be helpful to see this *dynamis* word defined as **God intentionally putting forth strength and ability from His moral excellence and resources.**

The word "perfect" in this passage is the Greek word *teleo*, meaning to fulfill or accomplish its purpose. What does God use to accomplish His purpose?_____

Some translations use the word "infirmity," but the Greek word for "weakness" here means the need for strength in the body and/or the soul due to various reasons. Is there any time we are not in need of strength of body and/or soul?

There is a bigger lesson here than just Paul's struggle with a "thorn in his flesh". God is making a powerful statement to us today. In every need, every lack, every situation, God intentionally brings resources from His very nature to accomplish all His purposes in us. The outcome may not always be as we hope or desire, but God is the ultimate recycler: He never wastes anything and has an endless supply for whatever we face every day: thorn or struggle, worry or wrinkle, crises or cries - He is powerfully eager to be powerfully known and experienced in every circumstance. **Our weaknesses, infirmities, struggles and strains are the framework for His power, His mighty strength, to be experienced according to His character and purposes.**

This word *dynamis* is also found in Ephesians 3:20-21 and Colossians 1:29. Where does Paul state the *dynamis* of God is mightily working?

_____

When Paul was writing to the Colossians, he was addressing some of the theological errors and concerns of this young house church. They were experiencing pressure to do human works of religious activity and severe self-discipline and avoidance of indulgence in order to be saved and/or be acceptable to Christ. Given this situation in Colossae, and their understanding of Paul's educational and experiential credentials, why do you think it was important for Paul to emphasize the *dynamis* of God mightily working within him?

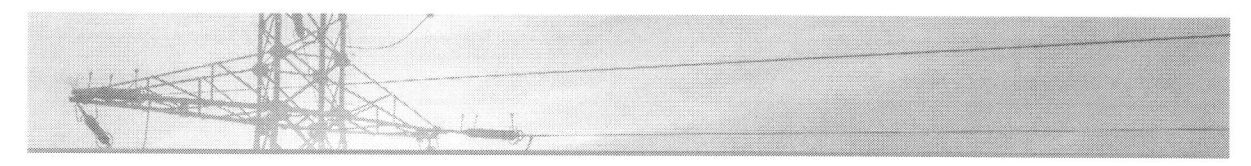

_____

_____

We may be tempted to think we have something more to add to what Christ has done, some "power" or strength or ability of our own that will bring about God's acceptance or plans. Truly we bring all that we are when we give our lives to Him, and He loves every aspect of our created being, including our inherent talents and abilities; but the good that God intends, the eternal impact that is potentially ours, will have more to do with the *dynamis* of God mightily working within us than any natural talent or ability. God is not increasing our human strength or ability, but giving us full access to His, by His power working within us.

One of my favorite quotes from Corrie Ten Boom (a Nazi prison camp survivor who became a legendary evangelist) says, "It's not my ability, but my response to God's ability, that counts."

This seems to be one of the themes of Paul's letters to the churches, for this is what he says to the Corinthians: "For God, who said, 'Light shall shine out of darkness,' is the One who has shone in our hearts to give the Light of the knowledge of the glory of God in the face of Christ. But we have this treasure in earthen vessels, so that the surpassing greatness of the power will be of God and not from ourselves (2 Corinthians 4:6-7)."

Yes, that is our word *dynamis* again. God's excellence is revealed in us "earthen vessels" through His power working within us. But we see in the very next verses that this doesn't mean all is peachy or without struggle - 2 Corinthians 4:8-9: "We are afflicted in every way, but not crushed; perplexed, but not despairing; persecuted, but not forsaken; struck down, but not destroyed."

We may struggle in profound ways, but God's power keeps us from being crushed, despairing, and forsaken or destroyed, because He is always working for our good, as we see in Romans 8:28-29. Although it is easy to try to tell God what we believe the "good" should be, part of maturing in Christ is allowing Him to define "good" for us and cooperating with the process of this "good" coming about, no matter what I'm facing today.

What ultimate good do you see in Romans 8:29?

_____

Selah.

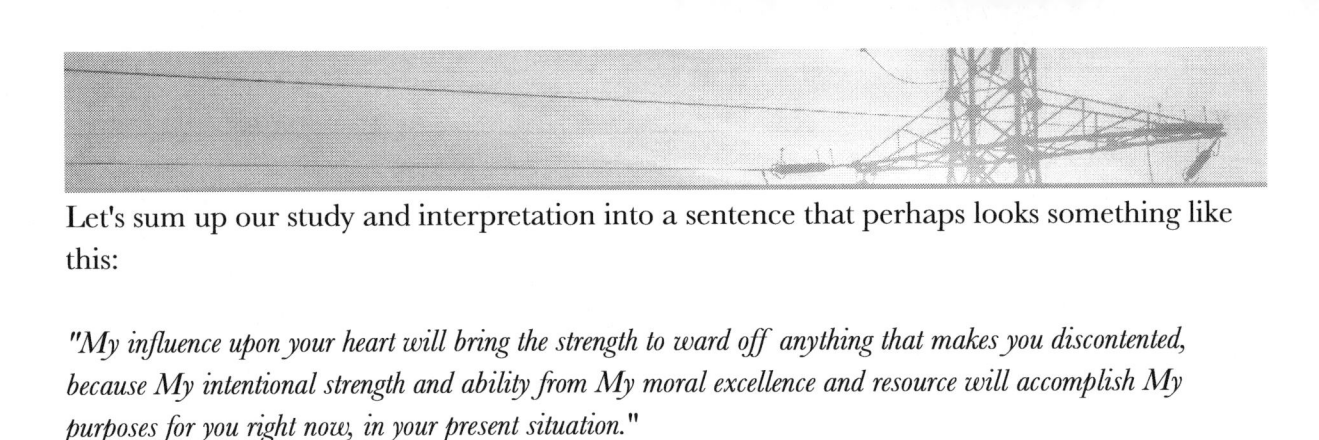

Let's sum up our study and interpretation into a sentence that perhaps looks something like this:

"My influence upon your heart will bring the strength to ward off anything that makes you discontented, because My intentional strength and ability from My moral excellence and resource will accomplish My purposes for you right now, in your present situation."

That's a long interpretation for a short verse, but I find this deeply encouraging and I hope you do too. We will experience the power of God in and through us as He intended when we choose to agree with what He is saying in this precious, powerful passage and then take action on our agreement. Agreeing with Him in prayer would be one practical step you can take today. Write out your prayer below, and also list other practical steps that may come to mind:

_____

_____

_____

On day 11 under the power lines God said: "It takes humility to receive My power, an agreement with Me that your power is weak and insufficient. Only through humility will My power flow - the bended knee and humble heart, the submitted mind and soul will be a conduit I can trust and use."

Given our study with Paul, why do you think humility is needed to be a useful conduit for His power to flow in and through us? (A hint can be found in James 4:6)

_____

_____

_____

Write out Philippians 2:8

_____

_____

_____

May we follow you in every way, Lord Jesus.

A suggested prayer for us as we close this lesson today

Lord God, today I humbly choose to confess my weakness and need to you. I hear You say You will bring the grace and influence upon my heart to be strengthened, the inclination to believe You, the resolve to receive Your power, and help to cooperate with the good You are bringing about in my life. I say "yes" to You today. I receive, my grateful heart receives Your all-sufficient power to rise above my situation. Today I choose to stand upon Your words with You. Thank you, my gracious, powerful God. Amen.

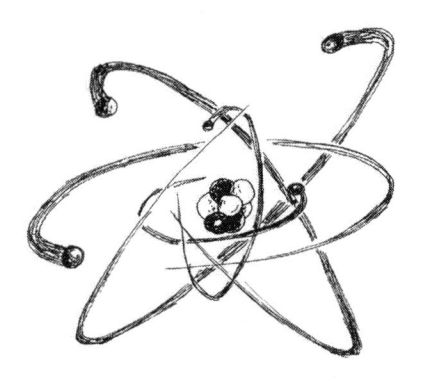

Chapter Three
The Power to be Held Together

On the fourth day under the power lines...I realize this may be starting to sound a bit like the Twelve Days of Christmas, but I promise you we won't be looking at each of the 101 visits under the power lines, for we would be here quite a long time. I noticed He would often repeat Himself to me under the power lines, knowing that would be the best technique with my particular attention span so I would truly "get it". So I've asked that the Holy Spirit pick and choose the direction of each lesson, whether it followed the chronological order of those 101 visits or not.

For instance, the fourth day under the power lines God said, "My power is My provision: It flows whether it is seen or not, but it cannot be of help if there is no connection to it." But on day eight, God spoke of this provision a little more specifically: "My power is absolute - pure, raw, untouchable. It would completely annihilate if I so chose. No human being can touch My power - they would be "undone," for the word of My power holds all things together. To receive My power is to receive restoration, sustaining enablement and transformation. No one who receives even one touch of My power stays the same. Yet to 'connect,' I must provide a protected way. I reach to you and you respond. I offer, you accept. I pour, you receive. I am, you will be."

Again on day 32, He said, "I hold all things together by the word of My power. I am the 'glue' of the universe. There is power for togetherness - internally, socially, spiritually, in every way."

Today we'll look at how He holds us together, both personally and as a community. He is so good. This lesson is a little long, so take a deep breath. Let's dig in.

A suggested prayer as we begin

Lord God, today I choose to focus as You direct me, to open my heart and mind to be taught by Your Spirit through Your word. I accept and I receive. Thank you. In Jesus' name, amen.

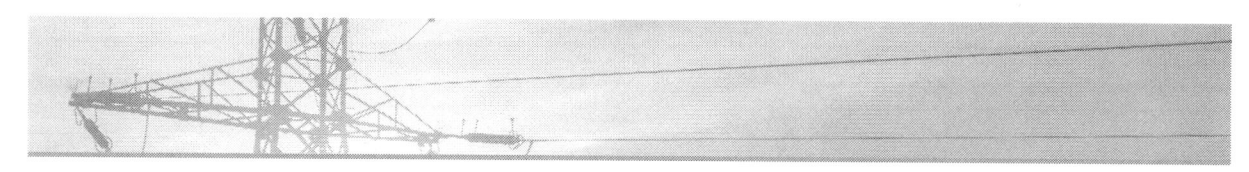

The phrase "My power holds all things together" comes from a passage from Hebrews 1:1-3. God knew that hearing this phrase under the power lines would spark a thought about that passage, so let's unpack it together.

Who is Paul speaking about in this passage? _____. (Verse 2)

Verse 3 gives two descriptions of Him. List them below:

1 - _____

2 - _____

What does verse 3 say Jesus is doing and how is He doing it? _____
_____

The meaning of the word "uphold" is to carry the burden, to keep it from falling. Some theologians believe that the meaning here is to "preserve," and from that thought they call Jesus the "Preserver of the Universe". That seems fitting in light of verse two, doesn't it?

How does Colossians 1:15-17 support this idea of Jesus as the Preserver of the Universe?
_____
_____
_____

These verses clearly state that Jesus holds all "stuff" together, everything. Let's go scientific for a moment. In the July 2000 online edition of Discovery Magazine I found this quote: *"You do not know what stuff is, you who hold it in your hands. Atoms? Yes, stuff is made of atoms. And every atom is a nucleus orbited by electrons. Every nucleus is built of protons. Every proton is - but there you reach the end of the line. Inside the proton lies the deep, unsettling truth: Stuff is made of nothing, or almost nothing, held together by glue, lots of glue. Physicists first began to suspect this in 1973. Lately it has been proved by experiment."*

The article is long and a bit technical, but you can read more of it here:
http://discovermagazine.com/2000/jul/featgluons

Here is the ending conclusion of the article: *As physics evolves, the image of the proton that quantum chromodynamics has given us may come to seem reassuringly concrete and solid—although solid is just what a proton is not. Flying into one—if you can imagine doing that, riding the strong force in a kind of subnuclear glider—would be like falling through Earth's atmosphere. The upper atmosphere of the proton is a thin cirrus of virtual quark-antiquark pairs; they form a shield for what lies below. As you fall past them, the atmosphere gets denser and denser, the clouds thicker and thicker. Your plane is struck with increasing frequency and force by flashes of color lightning—the gluons. And then, perhaps four-fifths of the way through your descent, you emerge from the cloud cover. The ride is calmer now. The lightning bolts have not disappeared; they have fused to a continuous sheet, and somehow you feel at once feather-light and immune from all forces. You're near the center of the proton now, utterly trapped as you fall toward the asymptote of utter freedom, and you are finding . . . not much.*

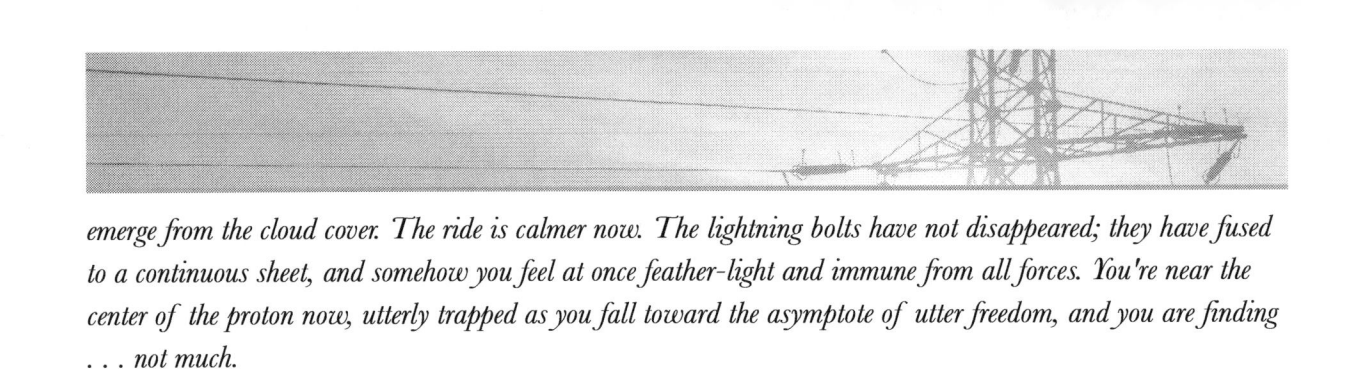

"The closer you look, the more you find the proton is dissolving into lots of particles, each of which is carrying very, very little energy," says Wilczek. "And the elements of reality that triggered the whole thing, the quarks, are these tiny little things in the middle of the cloud. In fact, if you follow the evolution to infinitely short distances, the triggering charge goes to zero. If you really study the equations, it gets almost mystical."

Yup, mystical it is. Science may help define quarks and anti-quarks, gluons and scientific color, revealing information as we observe it. But truly the "glue" that holds this all together would be Jesus Christ Himself.

How does He hold all things together according to Hebrews 1:3?

"...by the_____

The word "power" here is once again the *dynamis* of God. Review the meaning of *dynamis* in your own words: _____

_____

The Greek word for "word" here is *rhema*, which means that which has been or is spoken by a living voice, as opposed to a written word. In the Old Testament, the Hebrew word *amar* is similar to *rhema*. *Amar* is first found in Genesis 1:3. Write out the first three words of that verse here:_____

_____

When the Living God speaks something, it is eternal and lingers throughout time. It always accomplishes His intentions for speaking it, always works until it is accomplished. As an example, do we have the light that God spoke into existence? Since the sun and moon were not created until the 4th day, what could be the light that God spoke of on day one? Revelation 22:5 gives a clue.

Note your thoughts here: _____

_____

_____

So when God said, "Let there be light," could it be that He was saying, "Let Me be seen"? When God speaks, it continues until it is done. He delegated His light to the sun and moon for an era of time but then it will all go back to His light alone, as it was in the beginning. He will be seen!

What did Jesus call himself in John 8:12

He always fulfills what He says, in the Old Testament or in the New, in the old covenant or in the new, in creation or in our lives. He speaks and creates the universe and He speaks and comforts His child. His words linger, accomplishing His intentions as they resound throughout time. With a word the universe is held together and without that word it would fly apart.

Sounds a bit like our human souls, doesn't it? The living words of Jesus can hold us together, but apart from Him and His power it all seems to fly apart.

During a particularly painful time of loss and grief, I stood in my walk-in closet one morning trying to decide what to wear. Even that simple decision seemed too much for me, as I doubled over in grief and loss, dissolving into tears. I could tell the toll on my body was tremendous as I had been crying and grieving the loss of our son, and my soul felt as if it was "flying apart". As I cried out that day I told God that unless He helped me I would probably die of grief. I suspect you have had moments, or even seasons, where grief and/or loss or something doubles you over and you cry out just to survive it.

The good news is that He hears us, and is our very present help in time of trouble (Psalm 46:1). Somehow I straightened up and found some clothes and breathed my next breath. Somehow I took a step, and then one more. I didn't sense or feel anything unusual at the time, but the truth is that I was receiving help and power just to do those simple things. He held me together and will hold you, too. His strengthening power came to me and did help me. Otherwise I would still be in a sad puddle in my closet!

God reminded me under the power lines that we cannot connect with Him without His provision to do so, His words to "hold us together". Let's review this provision, His life-giving words:

Think a bit about the following words of Jesus and what He is offering you today. Pay particular attention to the "I am" statements that Jesus is declaring, and write them also.

Matthew 11:28-30

Matthew 28:16-20
_____
_____

John 6:35
_____
_____

John 8:12
_____
_____

John 10:9
_____
_____

John 11:25
_____
_____

John 15:1-11
_____
_____

When we receive His words, we are connecting with Him. And when we personalize scripture, we are engaging with Him in deeper ways. So to make this personal, go back over the "I am" statements of Jesus. Write in the space below, or elsewhere, a personalized acceptance of His declaration of His provision to you. Here is an example of this exercise using John 10:11-15: "Jesus, you are my good shepherd and you laid down your life so I may live. You know me and I know you, so I will continue on with you and you with me." Once you have finished writing these out, it would be particularly powerful to speak these statements out loud (shut the door; no one will mind).

_____
_____
_____
_____

When we find ourselves in need of the powerful "glue" of God, He is faithful to be with us, helping us as we go. Yet I believe His intention is to keep us "together" not just in a personal sense but also in the sense of community.

I was pondering this as I walked in our woods. Living in the woods in the Northwest is a tremendous gift, even in the rainy season, which we locals call just about every month except August. Yet it's stunningly beautiful here, even in the rain, even in storms. Watching our 150-foot-tall fir trees sway in stormy, heavy winds is something to behold. We've found that the limbs and trees and wet, soggy ground can lead to falling trees and debris, which can then lead to broken power lines somewhere. So when the power is off, we find candles, flashlights and whatever is needed to wait it out until the power comes back on.

We decided we would have a generator that we could start up in a power outage that would provide a measure of voltage so we could at least power up something to recharge or cook, or keep refrigerated. It's a relief to know we have the generator, especially since we get our water from our well, which uses an electric pump to get into the house.

A generator is a backup system for power to our house until our connections are restored. **I believe we are God's "backup system" for each other when there are broken connections for His power flowing to and through His people.**

I met with someone many years ago who was in great distress. We both agreed I was not her counselor, but rather a new friend with some spiritual insight (we both hoped so anyway). We met for a few times, and as she began to trust that I truly cared and listened, her painful past was shared and I wondered what to do.

Have you ever felt completely out of your league? I felt that way, but I cared about her so I hung in there. I could tell I had become emotionally involved because I dreamt that night that I was with her in one of the traumatic situations of her past and we were fighting off bad dudes and things all night. After I woke up I had a renewed conviction that we needed divine help. Some information came my way for a particular way to pray together, so I was all prepared for the next time we met. I love prayer strategies which can be a path to more wholeness and recovery. So we met and began to pray in a particular way.

But it wasn't "working". I couldn't quite figure out why, but we kept trying. Finally at one point we stopped that particular prayer strategy and simply sat together. Although the prayer strategy wasn't "working," His presence was very real with us in the room, a tenderness filling the air. Soon the tears began to fall, first hers and then mine. It was ok with her that I hug her, so I gave her a hug, and as I did I heard these words in my spirit: "This is the hug she should have received in those painful moments in the past."

At His direction I whispered this in her ear and more tears came, and along with them came a breakthrough of sorts which was an opening for healing. Something about that simple hug began the healing journey, including eventual helpful counseling and other resources. There were many parts to her healing journey, but it all began with a tender hug.

My friend had a "power outage" that was not of her own choosing. It just happened. Just as someone crashing into a power pole leaves the whole community without power, a traumatic event can disconnect us from the very source we need at the time of our greatest need. We can't seem to hear or sense God at all and feel alone and confused in the dark. Although the power is there, much like in power outages, the connections are broken.

And that is why we need each other. We are the "backup generator" for each other at times of disconnect from the needed power of God. We can sit with each other, pray for each other, help each other until we find our reconnection with God ourselves. It can be as simple as a divinely-directed hug or as dramatic as a divinely-directed intervention; but it's clear we are to be held together by the "word of His power".

On Day 99 under the power lines I heard, "Some circumstances make the need for My power obvious: tragedies; disasters; struggles; troubles; cold moments needing heat, the power of My warmth and light. But the truth is that all circumstances, all people, need Me - need the power I bring with My very presence. It's in the nature of man to forget this. Will you help them remember? Will you remember? I'm always here. Always."

As we learn to remember God's help and presence and reach out to each other, God can "hold us together" by the word of His power, as we learned earlier. He never intended that we live out our lives without community. He sets the lonely in families (Psalm 68), drawing us into His very own family! As we reach out to others our community is stronger, held together by the "glue" of Jesus Christ. The power of God comes to help us stick together, grow together, learn together, become better together.

What do the following verses tell you about living in His community, with one another?

Psalm 133

John 13:35

Romans 12:5

I Corinthians 12:12-20

Ephesians 4:16

Colossians 2:2

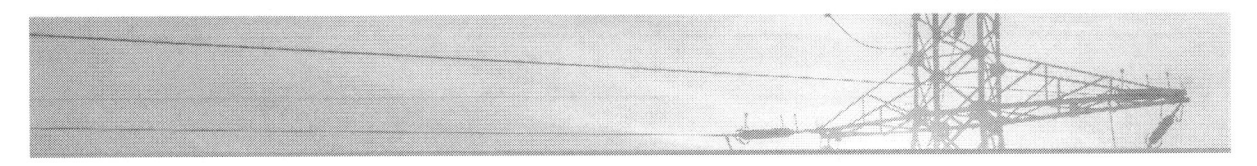

Jesus gave a command to His disciples, and to us, in John 13:14-15: "If I then, the Lord and the Teacher, washed your feet, you also ought to wash one another's feet. For I gave you an example that you also should do as I did to you."

On a website (gotquestions.org) I found this information about footwashing: "In Bible times, the dusty and dirty conditions of the region and the wearing of sandals necessitated footwashing. Although the disciples most likely would have been happy to wash Jesus' feet, they could not conceive of washing each other's feet. This was because in the society of the time, foot-washing was reserved for the lowliest of menial servants. Peers did not wash one another's feet, except very rarely and as a mark of great love."

Luke points out (22:24) that the disciples were arguing about who was the greatest among them, an attitude that precludes a willingness to stoop to wash feet. When Jesus moved to wash their feet...they were shocked. By washing His disciples' feet, Jesus taught the lesson of selfless service that was supremely exemplified by His death on the cross."

What could "washing one another's feet" look like for us today? Take a moment to think that over with the Lord, and write out your thoughts:

_____

_____

Are you willing to do this? _____

The joy of community together is part of our inheritance as His family, and it is also our responsibility as His family to be the "backup power system" for each other in hard times.

A caution to those who, by nature or experience, have a tendency to be "fixers" for others: Ultimately our purpose in coming alongside each other in times of "disconnect" is to facilitate God's love and presence and help, not create dependency on ourselves. Remember, in this analogy, generators are short-term backup systems until the connection can be restored. We always point the way to God with each other, whether in stormy "disconnections" or calm, balmy days. Sometimes it's taking the time to just show up for each other, sometimes it's as simple as what we say at the right time.

A few days after the loss of our son, I was standing in our entryway, perhaps to go out - I don't remember. But my brother, Scott, came in the door and stood in the entry with me, grabbed my shoulders, looked right into my eyes and spoke right into my soul. He told me to not let the light that is within me to go out, with other words of encouragement. I can still picture this moment in our entryway, and it still encourages me. A well-timed, heartfelt word washed more than my feet: It washed away thoughts of hiding and seclusion in my sorrow. It brought courage to stand until I could find a way to remember the song within my heart to keep standing.

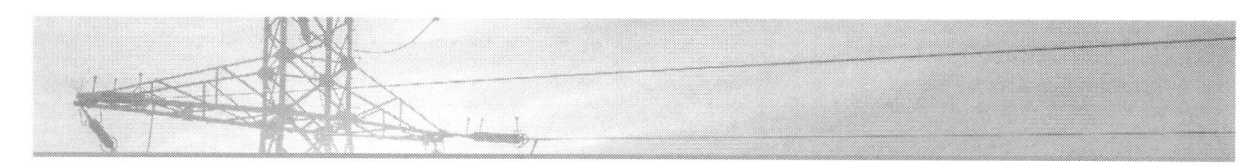

I found a little framed saying that I gave a friend who was struggling. It said, "A friend is someone who knows the song in your heart and can sing it back to you when you have forgotten the words (Anonymous)." I've often thought about that, particularly the moment when my brother "sang the song in my heart" for me in my entry way. But I've also wondered what it looks like in other practical ways.

What specific instructions do you see in these verses about living in His community together?

Romans 12:15-16

Philippians 2:1-11

Colossians 3:13

I Peter 3:8

Our culture promotes independence from others, and social media and other cultural devices seem to encourage and strengthen our distances and differences rather than our unity and community. But God's *dynamis* can hold us together as we cooperate with Him, singing words to each other that we've forgotten, standing with each other in joy and sorrow, listening and praying for each other, helping as He guides us. Whole regions can be affected if we'll do this.

How will the world recognize us as followers of Christ according to John 13:35?

On day 40 under the power lines I heard, "I connect people and network groups so My love is multiplied and My power is released into regions, places and seasons. The season is now. Be ready. There may seem to be no connection to local 'flows,' but the connection is there. Trust Me."

Okay, then. Let the singing and listening and praying and helping begin!

A suggested prayer as we close

Lord God, thank You for holding me together by Your kind goodness and power. And thank You for the way you hold us together in community. Forgive my indifference to my brothers and sisters around me. Forgive my neglect of the community You have given me. I believe You will give me Your power, Your divine energy to come alongside others to encourage and help as You direct and guide. Show me my next steps to connect with others in Your family. I agree with You that the season is now and I choose to be ready and useful, so Your love will be seen and known and the Kingdom will grow. In Jesus' name, amen.

Chapter Four

The Power of a Changed Heart

I don't remember the weather on day 34 under the power lines; but as I walked I usually looked around and studied the power lines and towers and other aspects of the area, rain or shine. This time I asked the Lord where to look and He replied, "Your heart." I asked Him what my heart had to do with it. He replied, "The heart has everything to do with it. It is the heart that holds the key to My power. Learn what is in My heart and choose to adjust yours. My power will flow according to the heart (mine and yours)." Then I asked Him how I "adjust" my heart. He replied, "You need My Spirit - you must cooperate by your choices each moment, each day. Seek Me, reach to understand. Ask Me. Knock - you know it will open. The choices to seek, ask, knock are the adjusting processes of your heart. Put what belongs to Me into your heart and life. Reject all other things."

I remember walking back to my house pondering this, wondering about my heart. Sometimes it's hard to know your own heart. I believe it takes some divine help and perspective. Today we'll look at God's heart and the process of adjusting our hearts, one of the keys to living a life of God's power.

A suggested prayer as we begin

Take as much time as you need with this one: Lord God, I ask that You help me see my own heart. I ask for the courage to see what You see, the focus and ability to realize what You may be saying to me. I receive Your power to adjust as You direct me. I know Your heart is trustworthy and ask that You make my heart like Yours. In Jesus' name, amen.

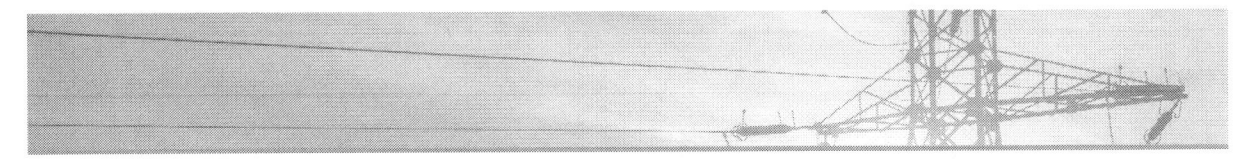

That was quite a prayer, but the adjustment process has already begun if you were willing to give it a shot. I'm on this heart journey with you, so let's explore some thoughts together.

We saw in chapter one that with God it's always about people, because He loves us, every single one of us. In fact, I John 4:7 says: "Beloved, let us love one another, for love is from God; and everyone who loves is born of God and knows God. The one who does not love does not know God, for God is love. By this the love of God was manifested in us, that God has sent His only begotten Son into the world so that we might live through Him."

John is boldly declaring that not only does God love us, God *is* love. He defines love by revealing it through Jesus - a living, breathing personification of Himself. That is why Jesus said that seeing Him (Jesus) is seeing the Father (John 14:9). And a good look at Jesus helps us see the loving heart of God. His thoughts and actions towards us can only come from His heart of love.

Choosing to believe this will help us in our pains and sorrows, questions and crises. If I choose to believe that God's heart is a heart of love, it becomes the filter through which I see and live my life. But the process of making this choice can sometimes be costly and difficult.

I had an experience some years after the death of our son that was so intimate and holy I didn't know if I would ever be able to talk about it. But at the time I asked God to give me the grace and words to share it, because it was such an important experience of God's heart. I've decided I would share it with you.

I was visiting a friend, staying in her mom's house, which had a lovely private swimming pool. My friend joked with me that it was like the "pool of Bethesda" (John 5), in that she had many spiritual experiences in that pool. So one afternoon I eagerly waded into the unknown, wondering if I, too, would have an experience. I had not been swimming since the drowning death of our son some years before, and I felt it was time.

I enjoyed myself, venturing into the deep end and swimming around. I wasn't paying attention to how tired I was getting, and suddenly realized I needed to get to the side of the pool before I sank. In that split-second moment of need, I found myself in that split-second moment of need of my son, struggling in the water at the lake near our home where he died.

I had never allowed myself to think about his struggle in the water. It was too hard; it took my breath away. In the pool that day in that moment, my heart constricted as if punched and I gasped, and then suddenly somehow found myself hanging onto the side of the pool, crying my eyes out.

I don't know how long I did that before a clear thought came to my mind, which I've learned to recognize as God's voice: "It was only a moment in time, a moment that Jeremy doesn't even consider now." I knew God was speaking about that moment of Jeremy's struggle in the water. But after I thought about what God said, I said, "Yes, but it's a moment in time I don't like." I immediately heard, "I don't like it either." Before I could even think about that, I then heard, "I didn't like it when you found out (that Jeremy had died) either..." And then began a shift, subtle at first but then definite: I went from the confines of my grieving heart to the expanse of God's grieving heart.

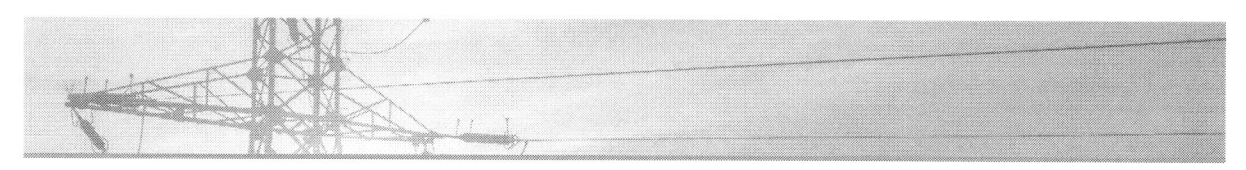

I don't know if you've ever considered how God feels about the pains and sorrows you've experienced. In the midst of a painful loss or crisis, it's easy to miss that in the theological confusion that can sometimes overtake us.

I hope my sharing a bit of this story will help you; because once this shift began, I heard Him share with me statements of His sorrow: that He didn't like it when others had been hurt, when events happened. It was as if He sped through history, revealing to this wet, dripping woman on the side of a pool a glimpse of His vast heart, longing for those He loves - us. When He got to how He felt about His own son hanging on the cross, I felt we were weeping together.

I was strangely comforted as we shared this time in the pool together. He didn't explain the many "whys" of Jeremy's death. He didn't give me His overall purpose and plans for such things. He simply opened His heart to me - a heart of love.

I don't know why God has chosen to organize the universe with an apparent selectivity of His involvement and actions with our free will and all that this means on our poor planet, but I have made a choice to believe in the vast, loving heart of God. I may not understand how His hands move or don't move, but I am coming to understand His heart for me, and for us - especially if we're a dripping mess.

Selah.

We saw in our previous studies that God's love is always in motion, doing or accomplishing something. For some of us who are "doers," action-oriented and outcome-based, God's apparent inaction at times is absolutely baffling. For some of us who are more relationally oriented, and perhaps emotionally based, God's apparent inaction at times is absolutely baffling. But let me assure you, no matter how you see it or what it looks like, God is always working (John 5:17), always accomplishing His purposes one step at a time, and always willing to share His heart of love with you. It's one thing to intellectually agree He loves you; it's another to let Him love you - to cooperate with His powerful work within us.

In the Old Testament He spoke of His promise to do this inward work in Ezekiel 36:26-27: "I will give you a _____ and put a new spirit within you; I will take the heart of stone out of your flesh and give you a _____. I will put my Spirit within you and cause you to walk in My statutes, and you will keep My judgments and do them."

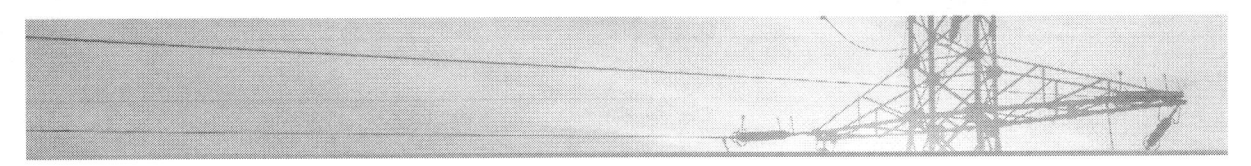

Many things and circumstances and choices can lead to a stony heart, but God promised a long time ago that He would take that heart and replace it with a heart of flesh, and would do it with His Spirit within us.

So then how do we cooperate with this process? My "choices" seem to be the key. Peter was very clear in Acts 2:38-39 that a choice must be made to repent and receive. "Peter said to them, 'Repent, and each of you be baptized in the name of Jesus Christ for the forgiveness of your sins; and you will receive the gift of the Holy Spirit. For the promise is for you and your children and for all who are far off, as many as the Lord our God will call to Himself.'"

I choose to repent (a change of mind that leads to a change of direction) and be baptized (immersed) in Jesus....and what do I receive at that time?

_____

_____

This is a promise for all, even those "who are far off". Note in verse 39: "...as many as the Lord our God will call to _____. Although we will have specific and personal assignments, truly our calling is to Himself, His power drawing us to His very heart.

So my first **key choice** is to repent and receive. The very first time I do this I become His child, a family member, and I'm given the Holy Spirit to dwell within, to remind me of all that Jesus has said and done, and all of the Kingdom ways of God. John 14:26: "But the Helper, the Holy Spirit, whom the Father will send in my name, He will teach you all things, and bring to your remembrance all that I said to you."

As I learn more and more of God's ways and Kingdom living, I will grow and need to make continual choices to have a change of mind that leads to a change of direction (repentance) and receive His power to take next steps. If you agree, write out a personal agreement with God about this:

_____

_____

Note what other key choices I can make to cooperate with the transformation of my heart from the verses below:

Ephesians 5:18 (MEV): "And do not be drunk with wine, for that is reckless living. But be filled with the Spirit." (Note: the phrase "be filled" is a present, passive, imperative verb, better translated as "keep on being filled".)

The choice I can make today:_____

_____

-36-

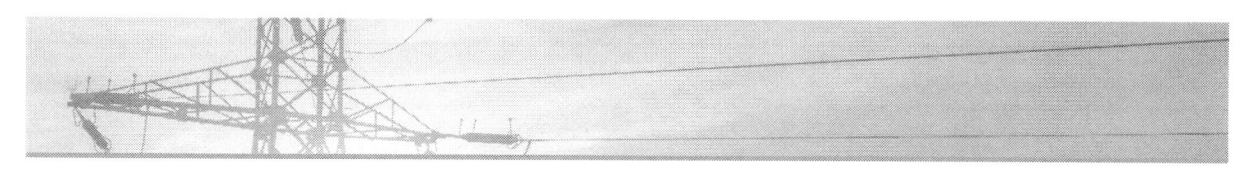

Ephesians 2:8-10 (NET): "For by grace you are saved through faith, and this is not from yourselves, it is the gift of God. It is not from works, so that no one can boast. For we are His workmanship, having been created in Christ Jesus for good works that God prepared beforehand so we may do them."

The choice I can make today:_____

_____

Matthew 7:7-11: "Ask, and it will be given to you; seek, and you will find; knock, and it will be opened to you. For everyone who asks receives, and he who seeks finds, and to him who knocks it will be opened. Or what man is there among you who, when his son asks for a loaf, will give him a stone? Or if he asks for a fish, he will not give him a snake, will he? If you then, being evil, know how to give good gifts to your children, how much more will your Father who is in heaven give what is good to those who ask him!"

The choice I can make today:_____

_____

I Peter 2:1-5 (ESV): "So put away all malice and all deceit and hypocrisy and envy and all slander. Like newborn infants, long for the pure spiritual milk, that by it you may grow up into salvation — if indeed you have tasted that the Lord is good. As you come to him, a living stone rejected by men but in the sight of God chosen and precious, you yourselves like living stones are being built up as a spiritual house, to be a holy priesthood, to offer spiritual sacrifices acceptable to God through Jesus Christ."

The choice I can make today:_____

_____

Colossians 3:1-5 (ESV): "If then you have been raised with Christ, seek the things that are above, where Christ is, seated at the right hand of God. Set your minds on things that are above, not on things that are on earth. For you have died, and your life is hidden with Christ in God. When Christ, who is your life, appears, then you also will appear with him in glory. Put to death therefore what is earthly in you: sexual immorality, impurity, passion, evil desire, and covetousness, which is idolatry..."

The choice I can make today:_____

_____

The Spirit-led choices I make are the key to a changed heart. If we will choose to cooperate with His work within us through His Spirit, we will find our hearts becoming more and more like His heart, caring about what He cares about.

Although my salvation at the time of my decision for Christ is immediate (called "justification" in Romans 3:24), the transformation of my heart and soul is not an immediate, automatic miracle. That is why we may see some who say they are Christian but their lives do not change. They have missed the beauty of cooperating with the process of a changed heart.

The process of this change is called going from "glory to glory" in 2 Corinthians 3:18: "But we all, with unveiled face, beholding as in a mirror the glory of the Lord, are being transformed into the same image from glory to glory, just as from the Lord, the Spirit."

The other word we sometimes use for this process is called "sanctification". 1 Thessalonians 5:23 says, "Now may the God of peace himself sanctify you completely, and may your whole spirit and soul and body be kept blameless at the coming of our Lord Jesus Christ." The Greek word for "sanctify" in this passage is *hagiazo*. This word has several meanings of being holy or being purified or set apart; but the usage in this passage specifically means, "to purify internally by reformation of soul". Our soul (which includes our mind, will and emotions) must go through the process of change to become like Him. My spirit came alive when I chose to give my life to Jesus, but my soul needs reformation to become like Him - a process He carefully guides by His Spirit. Jesus spoke about this in John 17:17.

What is Jesus praying we would be sanctified "in"? _____

The Greek word for "truth" here means simply what is true; but according to *Thayer's Greek Lexicon*, Jesus is using the word to specifically mean "the truth that is in Me and proceeds from Me." What three things does Jesus call Himself in John 14:6?

_____

Jesus identifies "truth" as a person - Himself. I know this can be a bit mind-boggling, but it will be worth it.

Looking again at John 17:17, what is the truth that sanctifies us?

_____

The Greek word for "word" here is *logos*. Its basic meaning is "speech". John was particularly deliberate with this word *logos* used in John 1:1 to help us see the Truth, describing Jesus as follows: _____

The Logos/Word of God has come to us, literally spoken to us through God Himself in the person of Jesus! I like the way The Message explains this in Hebrews 1:1-3: "Going through a long line of prophets, God has been addressing our ancestors in different ways for centuries. Recently He **spoke to us directly through His Son**. By His Son, God created the world in the beginning, and it will all belong to the Son at the end. This Son perfectly mirrors God, and is stamped with God's nature. He holds everything together by what He says—powerful words!"

When we understand this, we see that "truth" is far more relational than just data points or instructions or words on a page. We discover what is true through our relationship with Him, cooperating one choice at a time with the Word of God - Jesus. God has always intended that we would learn and grow by an ever-growing relationship with Him - even in the beginning in the garden of Eden. The sin-apple of bypassing the relational way of listening, following and learning severed the fresh and vibrant relationship with God - and the human heart began to become cold and stony. But God always provides a way back to Himself, drawing us with His great love - clearly seen in Jesus.

So our hearts do not have to remain cold and stony! Although there's effort involved and choices must be made, our great hope is in the Logos, the Word of God, Living Truth who came in human form, our Jesus, to powerfully redeem us and bring His power for a changed heart. Every once in a while it's ok to shout out your appreciation of this incredible saving work of God on your behalf, who brings life and beauty into our hearts and lives. Go ahead and shout it out, my friends! (Shut the door; no one will mind). Or perhaps write it out in the margin. It's good for our hearts to express our gratitude.

This deeper look at John 17:17 helps us see that Jesus was praying we would be reformed in our very hearts/souls by His own essence and presence and what proceeds from Him.

This dictionary definition may be helpful as we process this a bit more together:

> **proceed** - *verb*:
> [1] - to begin or continue a course of action. Synonyms: begin, make a start, get going, move, set something in motion.
> [2] - to move forward, especially after reaching a certain point. Synonyms: go, make one's way, advance, move, progress, carry on, press on, push on.
> [3] - do something as a natural or seemingly inevitable next step.

Paul wrote to the Romans about all things proceeding from Him in Romans 11:33-36. Verses 33-35 are shown here for you, but write out verse 36 on the lines below: "Oh, the depth of the riches both of the wisdom and knowledge of God! How unsearchable are His judgments and unfathomable His ways! For 'Who has known the mind of the Lord, or who became His counselor? Or who has first given to Him that it might be paid back to Him again?

"For _____

_____."

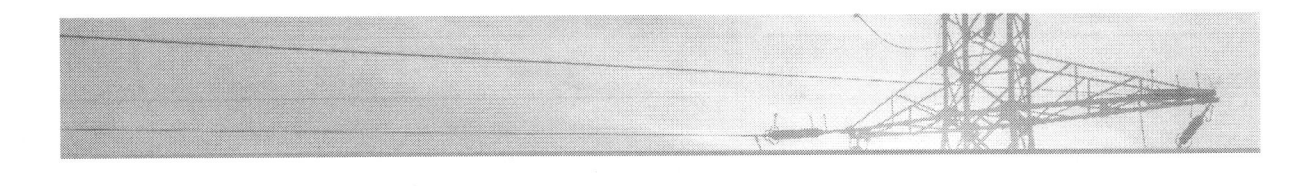

He doesn't just begin the process. It advances and progresses in Jesus, in our relationship with Him. It's natural for Jesus to reveal our next steps, and the beauty of it all is that He walks it out with us, the Holy Spirit within us revealing what we need as we study the scriptures and walk it out - one choice/step at a time.

The scriptures proceed from Him, inspired and protected by His Spirit, so what is written and revealed and spoken by His Spirit is worked out in my life as I walk in communion and cooperation with Him every day.

And what happens when I do this? My heart is changed, one choice at a time.

On day 84 under the power lines I heard, "Always go out under My protection, where My grace, mercy, kindness, strength and power first work within you, then through you to others....creating a fire of change and transformation in individual lives (starting with you) and in your families, your community, your area. Let Me work in you before you ask Me to work through you. This may take a long season or mere moments, but this cannot be ignored. Do not miss this key to My powerful presence and work."

It's a cooperative process. Perhaps another way of understanding the importance of this powerful work, this process, is found in Luke 6:43-45 (ESV): "For no good tree bears bad fruit, nor again does a bad tree bear good fruit, for each tree is known by its own fruit. For figs are not gathered from thorn bushes, nor are grapes each tree is known by its own fruit. For men do not gather figs from thorns, nor do they pick grapes picked from a bramble bush. The good person out of the good treasure of his heart produces good, and the evil person out of his evil treasure produces evil, for out of the abundance of the **heart** his mouth speaks."

Here's to good fruit proceeding abundantly from powerfully changed hearts!

A suggested prayer as we close

Today I choose to cooperate with You, Lord. I choose to go from glory to glory, growing more and more good treasure in my heart so I can speak words of life and love as I go. Thank you for sharing Your heart with me. Thank you for working within me. Thank you for a life of love and goodness. In Jesus' name, amen.

Chapter Five

The Power to See with Spiritual Eyes

On day 36 under the power lines I heard, "There is no limit to My power. Your eyes can only see a certain distance; your ears certain sound(s); your senses have limitations. Develop the discipline of sensing my intentions (I will always guide you) and trusting My power to accomplish it. Do not look with your natural senses. Only the Spirit within you can reveal and remind and rejuvenate with My power. The only thing I destroy is evil - the work of the enemy. Everything else I transform."

Again on day 39 He said, "It's important that you learn and understand My ways, how I work and how My power is displayed. My intentions are always expressed in My love, but it would be easy for your flesh to misinterpret my intentions. Listen closely and make no presumptions. See with your spirit, submitted to and filled by My Spirit - not your eyes. Don't let what you 'see' with your natural eyes discourage you. I'm always working."

Today we'll get a bit deeper into understanding this cooperative process within so we can "see with our spiritual eyes."

A suggested prayer as we begin

Lord God, I am used to seeing with my natural eyes and understanding, so I ask You to help me understand the process of seeing with my spiritual eyes, seeing what You see. I open my heart and mind to all that You have to teach me. In Jesus' name, amen.

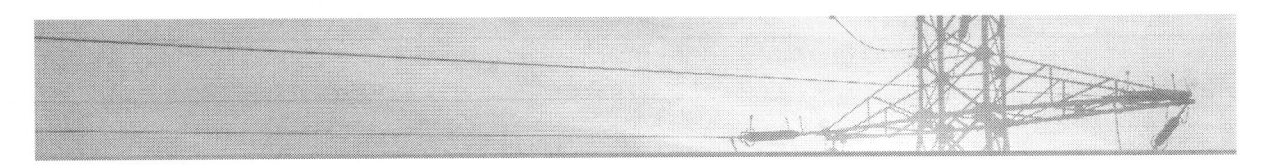

On day 83 as I stood outside during a beautiful sunny morning under the power lines, I told the Lord that it was beautiful there. I heard, "I want you to see with spiritual eyes - see Me and see what I see, and move as I direct you. As you go deeper with Me, you will naturally experience My power - it will amaze you."

I remember the first time I finally went to see an ophthalmologist for my eyesight issues. I had been putting this off for a long time, but eventually realized the fuzziness of the world needed some attention. After we diagnosed the issue and I filled my prescription for my glasses, I picked out frames that suited me and put them on. As I looked outside I distinctly remember thinking, "Good Lord - those trees have actual leaves!" And everything was so clear and sharp. I wondered why I had waited so long. Well, to be honest, I knew it had something to do with not wanting to wear glasses, but I found the same great delight in my eventual contact lenses. I was so grateful for the renewed ability to see more clearly.

A similar thing happened to my spirit when I "saw" Jesus in the sweet, glowing face of my older sister, Deb, after she had made a personal decision for Christ. We had both been raised in a denomination that taught Bible stories to us as children, but for some reason up to that point I had never heard about making a personal decision to receive Christ.

What is over the heart/eyes of those who don't know Christ according to 2 Corinthians 3:14?

When I noticed the change in Deb's very countenance, I began to search and seek and wonder. Although I didn't realize it at the time, the "veil" was lifting slowly but surely from my eyes. Seeing the light of Jesus in her caused me to want to find out more, and the hunger grew within me to "see God" for myself.

Matthew 5:8 says, "Blessed are the pure in spirit for they shall see God." The word "pure" in this verse is the Greek word *katharos* which means clean, pure, clear. The usage of *katharos* in this verse is speaking of ethically clean or pure; in other words, free from sin and guilt, free of anything false.

Did any red flags start flapping before you in the strong wind of the meaning of these words? Any thoughts that there is no way you could possibly be "pure" or "clean" from sin and guilt? Those listening to Jesus on the hill that day may have thought something similar. But let me remind you of the good news, the gospel of Jesus. It is His righteousness that God sees in you when He looks into your heart, now filled with the Holy Spirit, the Spirit of Jesus. Once we have made a personal decision to give Him all our sin and brokenness, He gives us His righteousness because of this amazing new covenant agreement in Jesus. He now sees this within us and says our spirit is "pure".

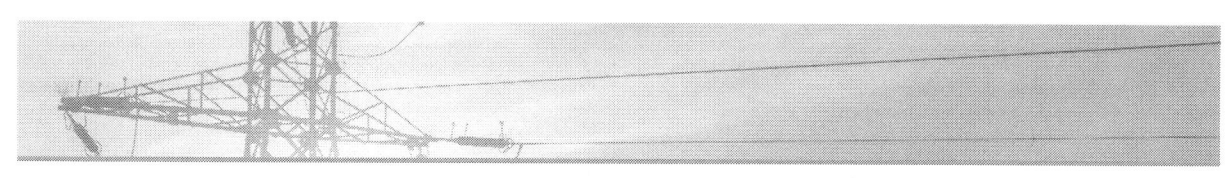

I realize this may feel like a stretch to you, but perhaps this explanation will help. The word "see" in this verse is the word *horao*, which has several meanings depending on its usage. The usage in this verse means "to see, i.e., become acquainted with by experience; to experience." So here's one possible interpretation of this encouraging verse: "Blessed are those who have had their hearts made clear and clean in Jesus, for now they will experience God." God's heart beats to be in restored relationship with us so that we will have a personal experience with Him. It was always His intention that we grow in our relationship and experience with Him every single day - truly "seeing" Him.

Yes, we may falter and fail and flail around with various choices and decisions. But He will clearly but kindly bring us back to right decisions and the right direction to walk with Him each day. He will never call the Holy Spirit within you "impure". So, beloved child of God, you are pure in heart and you can experience God. Selah.

Our **first step** in the cooperative process of seeing with our spiritual eyes is to write out our agreement with God from Matthew 5:8

_____

_____

Because this is true, Paul wrote to the Christians in Ephesus these interesting words: Ephesians 1:18-19 (NIV): "I pray that the **eyes of your heart** may be enlightened in order that you may know the hope to which He has called you, the riches of His glorious inheritance in His holy people, and His incomparably great power for us who believe."

The phrase "eyes of your heart" is figuratively speaking of the eyes of the mind, the faculty of knowing something "deep within" you. The word for "enlightened" in this verse is *photizo*, which figuratively means to enlighten spiritually; to instruct, to inform, to teach, to give understanding. **Seeing with spiritual eyes, therefore, means choosing to focus and grow in my ability to understand spiritual realities.**

What are the three spiritual realities Paul prays will be known and understood if we'll have the **eyes of our heart** within us instructed, informed and taught?

1. _____
2. _____
3. _____

The word "hope" in this passage is the Greek word *elpis*, from a root word meaning anticipating in a good or pleasurable way, and could be interpreted as "glad expectation". Some versions phrase this part of the passage as "the hope of your calling". Some have said that this hope, this glad expectation, is the Lord's hope - His glad expectation about us. As we've already studied, we are first and foremost called into the embrace of His salvation through Jesus Christ.

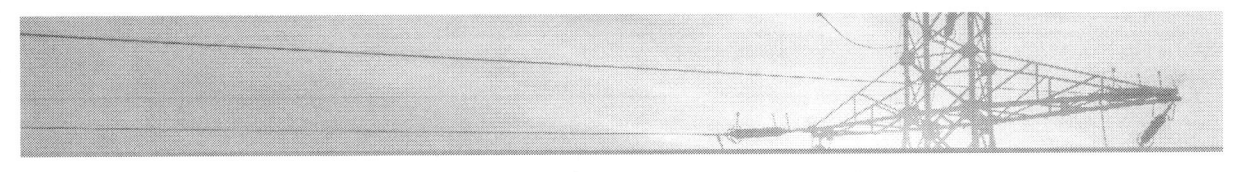

We'll look in later lessons into the truth that He calls us into partnership with Him on earth to walk out this salvation to further the Kingdom. Why do you think it would be helpful for us to deepen our understanding of Jesus' glad expectation about us?

_____

_____

It would be easy to miss some interesting wording in verse 18 - the "glorious riches of *His* inheritance in the saints." I italicized a word that I've often missed when reading this in the past. Considering this word, whose inheritance is Paul speaking about?
_____.

The word "riches" (Greek word *ploutos*) can mean "wealth," but the usage here means "fullness, abundance." There are many ways to look at what Paul is saying here, but consider the abundance of what is offered us through Christ as an "heir" of God (Galatians 4:7). Why would deepening our understanding of this be helpful?

_____

_____

_____

I found this bit of interesting information on the bible.org website: *Warren Wiersbe (Be Rich, pp. 13-14) writes, "When she was young, Victoria was shielded from the fact that she would be the next ruling monarch of England lest this knowledge spoil her. When her teacher finally did let her discover for herself that she would one day be Queen of England, Victoria's response was, 'Then I will be good!' Her life would be controlled by her position. No matter where she was, Victoria was governed by the fact that she sat on the throne of England. Even so, we will reign with Christ! Knowing that, we should live as His special people. Young Victoria had her eyes opened to her future, and when that happened she adjusted her life accordingly. We can do this too."*

I like the way The Message interprets this passage. Ephesians 1:15-19 - "That's why, when I heard of the solid trust you have in the Master Jesus and your outpouring of love to all the followers of Jesus, I couldn't stop thanking God for you—every time I prayed, I'd think of you and give thanks. But I do more than thank. I ask—ask the God of our Master, Jesus Christ, the God of glory—to make you intelligent and discerning in knowing Him personally, your eyes focused and clear, so that you can see exactly what it is He is calling you to do, grasp the immensity of this glorious way of life He has for his followers. Oh, the utter extravagance of His work in us who trust Him—endless energy, boundless strength!"

This "endless energy, boundless strength" is described in the last half of verse 19 through verse 22. What did the power of God, the *dynamis* of God, do according to verse 20?

_____

The same power that raised Jesus from the dead is ours today, because the same God that raised Jesus also raises us to a life of glorious abundance with endless strength. We may agree with our minds that this is what scripture says, but how do we reconcile "glorious abundance" and "endless strength" when we feel we lack in both, perhaps even suffering in some way?

In Paul's letter of encouragement to Timothy, he addresses some of these issues while he was suffering for the gospel. Look at Paul's words in 2 Timothy 1:6-14. Paul reminds Timothy (and us) that God did not give us a spirit of _____, but through the Spirit gives us these three things:

1 - _____
2 - _____
3 - _____

Yes, that's our word *dynamis*, the power of God - given to us by the Spirit to ignite us, give us clarity and focus, even in suffering. Relying on the Spirit and the power He brings is a choice.

On day 60 under the power lines I heard, "Unexpected - Often people do not expect or anticipate My power because they are so used to their own strength and energy guiding them. Abandon yourself into My care and purposes in every way and see the surge, know the grace I will pour upon, in and through you."

It may seem counterintuitive to entrust yourself to an unseen God when suffering in some way; but perhaps that is even more true when we don't seem to need anything at all, blindly going through our days dependent upon our own power and resources.

We can choose to rely our own strength, or we can choose to rely on the "incomparably great power" Paul says is "for us who believe". I had quite a little journey of discovery with that simple word "for" us who believe. This is no small word in the Greek, for it apparently was one of Paul's favorite little prepositions. It's basic meaning is "denoting entrance into, or direction." It's used regarding a place, a time, or metaphorically where one thing is changed to the end which one has in view. Once again in this little word we see that **the power of**

God infuses the beloved child of God, bringing transformation for the beautiful purpose that God has in view. This is true whether we're suffering in some way, surging in our growing journey, or surfing along the waves of His provision.

Do you see it?

Take a look at 2 Corinthians 4:18: "So we fix our eyes not on what is _____, but on what is _____. For what is seen is temporary, but what is unseen is eternal."

You may already know that the word "fix" here is not just a passing glance. It is more like staring, turning away from other things to focus on one thing.

The admonition to fix our eyes on something is also found in Hebrews 12:1-3. Where are we told to fix our eyes?

_____

_____

We have a choice to make: Where we will fix our eyes, what will be our focus and attention? If I don't feel strong or powerful or like I'm frolicking around in abundance, I have a choice to make. I don't think Paul is telling us to not feel natural feelings or not see natural things. We need our natural faculties about us so we literally don't bump into walls. But these natural things are "temporary" in the big picture of what God calls life. When we choose to see with spiritual eyes, the Spirit helps us grow in our ability to see what God sees, to know what He wants us to know - to grow in our understanding deep within our "knower" so we are not discouraged by natural situations and events. We are encouraged by the brightness of His presence and guidance. We are stable with our eyes on Him as His power flows.

On day 76 I heard, "My power is released in, among, and through My people - those who are aligned with Me, those whose eyes are fixed on Me, those whose hearts are ready. Are you ready?"

Our **second step** in the cooperative process of seeing with our spiritual eyes is to make a choice to fix our eyes on Jesus. Write out what that means to you in the form of a prayer:

_____

_____

_____

_____

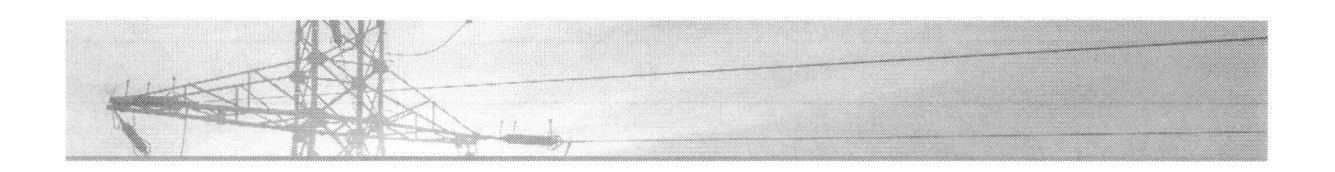

A suggested prayer as we close

Lord God, I choose to open my spiritual eyes and see You more clearly, see Kingdom things for what they are, see the big picture of my life. I thank you for giving me Your power to do this deep within me. I choose to focus and cooperate today. Help me to choose to focus and cooperate tomorrow. In Jesus' name, amen.

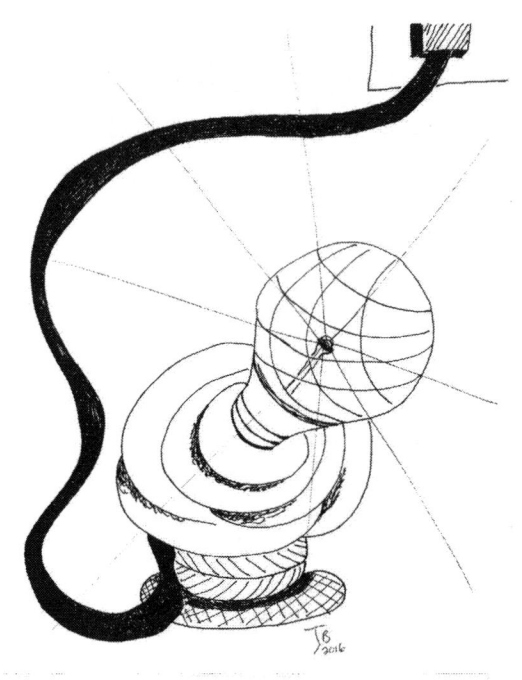

Chapter Six

The Power to Hope and Bring Hope

I had an interesting experience on day 55 under the power lines. I heard, "My power is DC but love and compassion converts/transforms it to AC, so it can be received. No 'fried circuits,' just transforming power. I love to see My love bring power to a broken life so that hope can flourish, enabling reception of change, the change I bring."

I have no electrical understanding or training other than "don't touch it," but this interesting reference to AC/DC power motivated me to do some studying. DC stands for "direct current" and AC stands for "alternating current". Of course He knew this would intrigue me, and I hope it intrigues you. I believe we are on to something important here. And so as we study the scriptures today and consider what He is saying to us, it would be a good idea once again to begin with prayer.

A suggested prayer as we begin

Lord God, I know that You have given me your Holy Spirit as my teacher, so I open my mind and soul again to Your teaching today. Help me grasp and understand the things of your Kingdom and cooperate with Your leading and guiding me today. I pray this in Jesus' name, amen.

Write out Psalm 147:5

_____

_____

_____

God's power is abundant, never changing and eternal, but our use of electricity is relatively recent. And apparently it wasn't until the 1950's that we started using AC power with the use of transformers. I found some information on a website (www.wisegeek.com) that helped me understand the difference between DC and AC power: "*Electricity is a type of energy that involves the movement of electrons along a conductor, such as a wire. The flow of electrons can occur in one direction or both directions along the wire. When electricity flows in one direction, it is referred to as direct current (DC). Alternating current (AC) is when the electrons flow in both directions — one and then the other. Batteries produce direct current, and electrical power grids that provide electricity to homes and other buildings use alternating current.*"

One of the other main differences between AC and DC is voltage, and the distance it can travel: "*Transformers are used wherever an electrical voltage needs to be increased or decreased. For example, they are commonly seen on electrical poles. A power plant produces electricity at a very high voltage so that it can travel great distances. The voltage must be reduced, however, before the electricity reaches homes and other buildings that use it to power appliances, machinery and other devices.*" Too much voltage leads to dangerous consequences.

There are some sobering cautions for those working regularly with electrical current. (http://electrical-engineering-portal.com/what-psychological-effect-does-an-electric-shock). The "zapping" pain of having contact with minimal voltage is the least of your worries. According to this website, it's the very real danger of contact with live high voltage that can be devastating to human beings - who also have "'*electrical current' transmitters in the form of neurons which process and conduct the multitude of signals responsible for regulation of many body functions. The brain, spinal cord, and sensory/motor organs in the body function together to allow it to sense, move, respond, think, and remember. Nerve cells communicate to each other by acting as 'transducers' creating electrical signals (very small voltages and currents) in response to the input of certain chemical compounds called neurotransmitters, and releasing neurotransmitters when stimulated by electrical signals.*"

As I studied this basic scientific information I began to marvel at God's referencing electricity as a powerful metaphor for His power, which is conducted not just through our power lines but through our ingeniously created human bodies. How clever of Him to ask us to meet Him "under the power lines," knowing the current that naturally and constantly flows through our bodies even this very moment.

We need electrical impulses to function properly in our bodies, as well as our homes. The electricity for some things in our homes needs to be transformed from DC to AC to be powered properly with the correct voltage. I suggest something similar happens for us in a spiritual sense. It's God's compassion and love for us that conducts His power in ways that are transformed to "appropriate" uses, just like DC is transformed to AC for appropriate uses in our homes.

How is God's love and compassion seen in the verses below?

Matthew 9:35-38

_____

Luke 9:1-6

_____

Luke 15:11-32

_____

List the changes that occurred due to God's transforming power expressed through His love and compassion in the verses above:

_____

_____

_____

Remembering that hope is the Greek word "*elpis*", meaning glad expectation, do you think those affected in the verses above had any change in their "glad expectation" of the future? If so, why?

_____

_____

_____

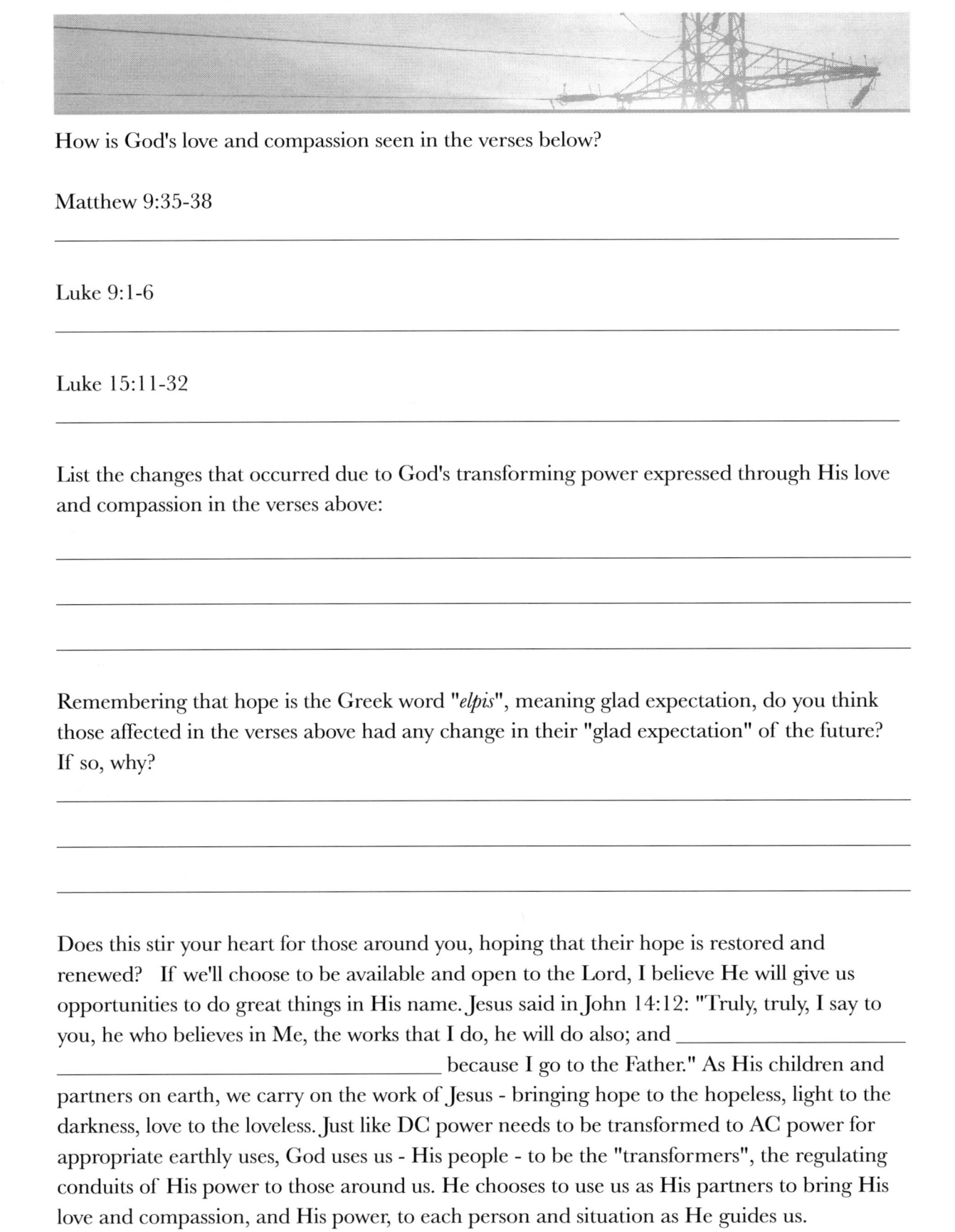

Does this stir your heart for those around you, hoping that their hope is restored and renewed? If we'll choose to be available and open to the Lord, I believe He will give us opportunities to do great things in His name. Jesus said in John 14:12: "Truly, truly, I say to you, he who believes in Me, the works that I do, he will do also; and _____ _____ because I go to the Father." As His children and partners on earth, we carry on the work of Jesus - bringing hope to the hopeless, light to the darkness, love to the loveless. Just like DC power needs to be transformed to AC power for appropriate earthly uses, God uses us - His people - to be the "transformers", the regulating conduits of His power to those around us. He chooses to use us as His partners to bring His love and compassion, and His power, to each person and situation as He guides us.

We'll study this concept of partnering with God in a later lesson; but the concept of the importance and value of our cooperation, so that His power can be experienced and hope can flourish, is a vital part of understanding how God's power works on the earth. We are the conduits and "transformers," if we'll choose to stay and learn and move as He directs. It's a process that involves making a choice to "make room for hope," a quote I heard recently by Eric Spangler (Asia Director for Free Methodist World Missions). In a gathering of pastors and leaders, Eric encouraged us to make sure there are no "pinch points" to the flow of hope, the flow of God's power through us. Addressing the issues that may be these "pinch points" will be uncomfortable, but if we are wanting the power of God to flow in and through us, we have a choice to make to learn and grow in the process.

That process of learning and moving as He directs is described in Romans 5:1-5. List the progression described this passage below:

"Therefore, having been

1 - _____ we have peace with God through our Lord Jesus Christ, through whom also we have obtained our introduction by faith into this grace in which we stand;

2 - and we _____ of the glory of God.

3 - And not only this, but we also _____,
knowing that tribulation brings about...

    a: _____ and _____
                                                                                  (brings about...)

    b: _____ and _____
                                                                                  (brings about...)

    c: _____ and _____

does not disappoint, because the love of God has been poured out within our hearts through the Holy Spirit who was given to us."

There's our word "hope": the glad expectation of what is ahead, because of Jesus and the love and power of God working within us and through us. It's a choice to engage and be involved as a "transformer".

On day 31 under the power lines I heard, "Every day I provide opportunities for My people to be conduits of My transforming power. Each expression and manifestation is unique, but My power is constant. One moment leads to another. Stay, learn and move as I direct. It will spill over, run down, change lives, grow the Kingdom...all in close relationship and communication with Me."

The choice we make to learn and grow and be a conduit, a transformer, of His power is made every day, on good days and on bad days.

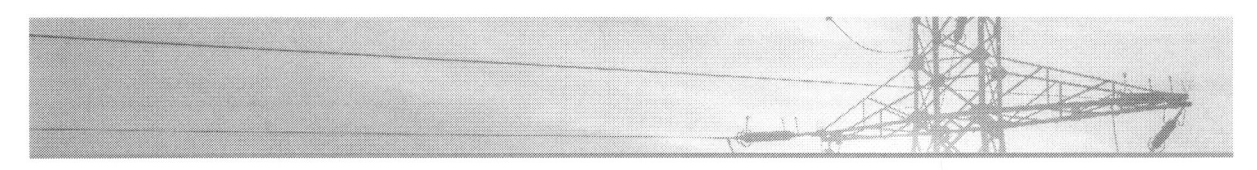

On day 90 under the power lines I heard, "So many who love me and call on my name still choose to operate in their own power, being convinced that it is enough. Only when faced with things bigger than themselves do they realize their own power is woefully inadequate. But those who are familiar with My ways and aware of their human frailties and limitations, who cry out to Me and remember My very essence, the power of My being - those ones find Me and are transformed, shaped, usable and listening. I am looking for these ones. Are you one of these?"

Since it is truly up to me whether I am "one of these" or not, it is my glad expectation (hope) that I am. When my "glad expectation" in my own power fails, I am ready to experience "glad expectation" in the power God applies from His abundant goodness and resources. And when I do that, I am well positioned to be the loving, helpful and hopeful presence that those around me need.

So let's get practical. What changes are you hoping for that God's power, expressed through His love and compassion through you, could accomplish? If you are willing, take a moment to pour out your heart to God and anticipate His presence with you with glad expectation. Write out your prayer here:

_____

_____

_____

_____

_____

Now remembering that all of His children can hear His voice (John 10:27), and that He will never say anything to you out of condemnation or criticism, ask Him to speak to you. Write out what you may be hearing God say to you today. Remember, each of us may hear Him differently. Perhaps it will be a verse (in fact, He will most likely start there); or perhaps a song will come to mind, encouraging words, comfort, strengthening. Ask Him to speak to you, quiet your heart and mind, start writing, and see what happens. Then, like the Bereans (Acts 17:11), double-check what you've written with the scriptures. If it lines up with scripture, it most certainly is not the devil speaking to you. And although it could be your own thoughts, it could still be encouraging. David "strengthened himself in God" (I Samuel 30:6). Even so, we sometimes mistake the clear thoughts that come to our minds as our own or some other influence, when truly it is the Spirit of God working through our mind - His favorite place to work to bring transformation (Romans 12:1-3). Give it a shot:

_____

_____

_____

_____
_____
_____
_____
_____

God loves to use His family to bring encouragement to each other. Check these thoughts and words with a trusted friend or small group, and pray over them together.

A suggested prayer as we close

Father, we agree together in Your presence and in Your name. We add our hopes and prayers together, and choose to receive Your empowering help so that glad expectation can flourish, love can grow, and change can come. We thank you. In Jesus' name, amen.

Chapter Seven
The Power of Being Present in His Presence

We were kneeling in prayer together, huddled at the altar at our church, responding to the call to come forward for prayer "if you need it." We needed it. We were still in the early stages of grief over the loss of our son and we knew we needed all the help available to us.

As we knelt there I could hear people coming up to surround and support us. Prayers were said that I don't remember hearing, mainly because something began to happen. I felt a warmth start deep within me that began to spread out throughout my body. It was like warm oil, comforting and soothing. I've since come to understand that this was the peace of God because of the presence of God. Clearly our friends were praying for this for us. I'm so grateful for supporting friends who believe He holds all things together - both grieving families and the friends who pray for them.

I don't know why this was a particular manifestation for me at that time - there were other times of prayer where no such manifestation happened. I don't know why sometimes we find ourselves in a very real and unforgettable experience of God's presence, and other times we believe He is present and march on as best we can without any such experience. Yet a clear foundational truth stands out for us today - He is always powerfully present.

What is the main point of Psalm 139:7-11:

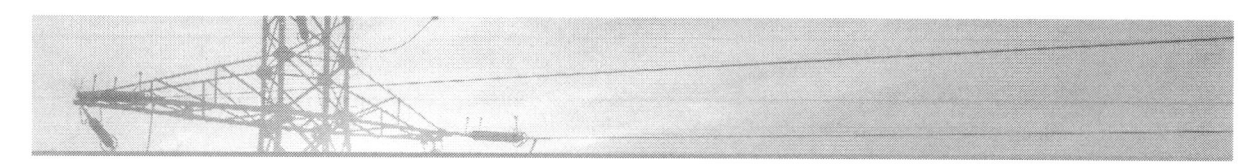

On day 56, I heard, "My power will always be experienced in My presence. Seek My face, hunger for My presence, reach for understanding and wisdom. Ask, knock, seek. I long to open the door of intimacy and fellowship with you so that we can accomplish My purposes on earth - where you live - right now - today."

Although it's true He is always present, perhaps we could say that we are not always "present" with Him - awake, alert and attentive. Today we'll look at some practices to be empowered to be present in His presence.

A suggested prayer as we begin

Lord, I ask for Your help today so I can grow in my understanding and knowledge of You. I choose to cooperate. Give me insight as I study. Help me remember that You are with me as my teacher and guide. In Jesus' name, amen.

I remember a quote (author unknown) that really stayed with me. It says, "The Bible is the only book where the author is always present when one reads it." So as we study today, He is with us - powerfully present to help us.

What do the following verses say about the presence of the Lord?

Psalm 16:11

_____

_____

Matthew 28:20

_____

_____

John 14:16-17

_____

_____

Acts 3:19-20:

_____

_____

Hebrews 13:5-6

_____

_____

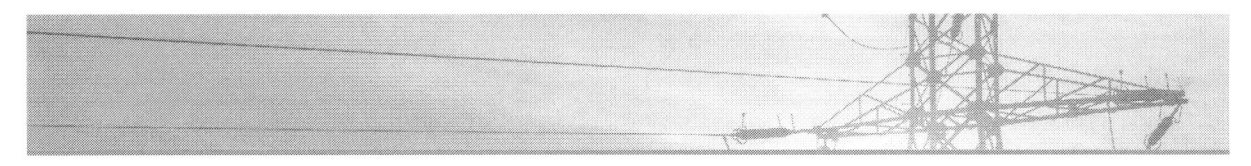

I John 4:12-16

It's one thing to study and read and even know in our "knower" that God is present with us, but it seems to be another thing to remember that and walk in His presence as we go. It doesn't seem possible to be in the presence of God and not know it, but unfortunately I've proven that it is possible. Perhaps you have, too. I've been distracted or even "numbed" to His presence many times. Many times I've not "felt" anything at all, and in some circumstances this can be disheartening, especially when others around you may be having tremendous experiences and you stand there wondering what is wrong with you. It's possible nothing at all is wrong with you; it's just the way it is at the moment.

Some of us are "wired" with personalities that are more analytical or more prone to the intellectual side of experiences. The "how" of something, or perhaps even the "why" of something, matters to us, and we may find that emotionally relating to others is a bit of a stretch at times. This may be the case in our relationship with God as well, since it is a relationship after all. Even so, let me encourage you that He is with you. His powerful presence is never just for others who seem to have special spiritual "antennae" or something that can sense His presence. For those of us who are wired in this way, we can choose to be "present," paying attention in the here and now, and walk in faith that He says He is with us and His presence is powerfully at work whether I feel it or sense it or not. Although He cares about how we feel, we will focus on Him, not on how we feel. It's a choice.

Some of us may be more relationally oriented, and therefore the relationship with God, although perhaps difficult at times, isn't quite such a stretch. We may have some "sense" or feeling of His presence, perhaps even a manifestation of some sort (e.g., shaking, a sense of warmth, goosebumps, etc.). Each of us is different and each of us experiences His presence differently. For those of us who are wired to perhaps feel His presence in more tactile ways, we will choose to be "present" - paying attention in the here and now and walking in faith that He is with us and His presence is powerfully at work regardless of our feelings or manifestations. Although He cares about how we feel, we will focus on Him, not how we feel. It's a choice.

On day 85 I heard, "My Church longs for My presence and cries out to me, but My Church only wants My comfort, not My power. My comfort meets them where they are. My power requires them to meet Me where I am and to be changed. My power is not a commodity to be measured out. It is My very being. I bring change - I am the Creator still. Will you cooperate? This is a season of change - renewal, revival, redemption. It's not about you, but it can be through you. Will you cooperate?"

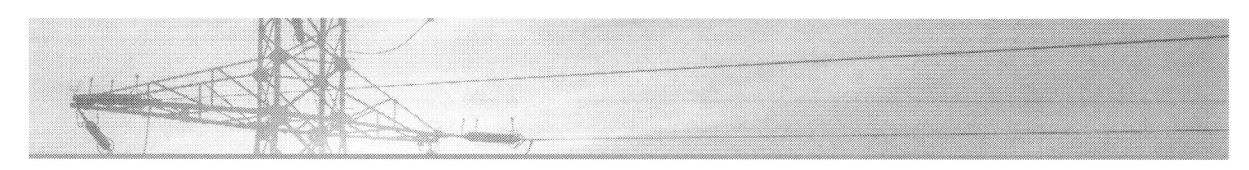

As we consider how to cooperate, I would like to suggest some empowered practices to help us be present - being awake, alert and attentive in the here and now - in His presence.

Practice #1: Preparing Myself. This involves laying down my distractions as well as my preconceived notions and ideas, and then opening my mind and life to Him. This may seem obvious, but it's amazing how often I have to remind myself to do this. On day 67 under the power lines I heard, "You cannot prepare for the cost, but you can prepare for being in My presence and power. Tell me everything and listen. I will counsel you, guide you, surround you, enable you, strengthen you, deploy your gifts, uphold My purposes in you - because I love you."

The lack of this particular practice may be the explanation of a situation described in Mark 6. Jesus was in His hometown teaching, and all that He had miraculously done and taught in other places was already rumored among the people. But they took "offense" at Him because all they could think about was their preconceived notions of Him, numbed and distracted as they were by their presumed familiarity and opinion. Verse five says (ESV), "And he could there do no mighty work, save that He laid His hands upon a few sick folk, and healed them." The phrase "mighty work" is our word "*dynamis*", the intentionally applied power of God. Why would their attitude be a hindrance to His power being manifested as He desired? Write out your first thoughts about that here:

_____

_____

_____

_____

As a grandmother, I find I have to restrain myself from just pouring out every adorable gift I see for my grandchildren. It wouldn't be good for them to be waking up every morning with gifts piled up around their beds as I would like. Although God has the power to pour out miracle upon miracle at any place at any time, He is more concerned with our hearts and our openness for a growing relationship with Him than any supernatural display. If we have no desire for Him, no preparation or willingness or openness to receive Him as He truly is, other than what we presume or even demand, He seems to restrain Himself knowing our participation and cooperation is an important part of our development and growth. He doesn't pull away from us, as some have perhaps accused, but waits for the heart that is open to Him.

But if I will choose this **practice #1 of Preparing Myself** and turn my heart and attention to Him, I'll find that I am present with the very Person whose presence is always with me. My willing heart is open to His always willing, open heart.

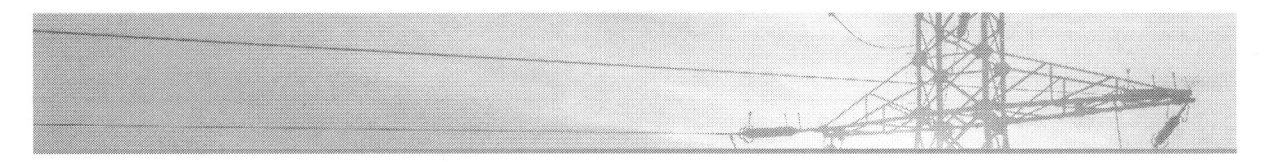

His heart can be seen in Luke 11:9-12 (NIV): "So I say to you: Ask and it will be given to you; seek and you will find; knock and the door will be opened to you. For everyone who asks receives; the one who seeks finds; and to the one who knocks, the door will be opened. Which of you fathers, if your son asks for a fish, will give him a snake instead? Or if he asks for an egg, will give him a scorpion? If you then, though you are evil, know how to give good gifts to your children, how much more will your Father in heaven give the Holy Spirit to those who ask Him!"

What does this passage call earthly fathers? _____
(Note: The Greek word for "evil" here does not mean demonic or other evil things that may have come to mind. We know there are good and kind fathers on the earth - but this word implies ethically "bad" nature with bad results, especially when compared to God.).

What does this passage call God?
_____

What will He give to those who ask Him?
_____

He is so willing to give, so generous in character and nature. He will give us His very person when we ask. For us in this "church age," that would be the person of the Holy Spirit.

But let's back up a bit in scripture:

What did God say to Abraham in Genesis 15:1?
_____
_____

Abraham was disappointed that he had not yet received his promised heir and was sulking in the "tent of his disappointment", a phrase I heard in a helpful sermon by Pastor Judah Smith in Kirkland, Washington some years ago. I can relate to this particular "tent"; how about you? God had to take him by the hand, pull him out of his tent, and have him count stars to get him to pay attention to the bigger picture and remember God's promises.

Although some versions say God told Abraham that his reward will be very great, or he will have a very great reward, a better translation of the Hebrew would be "I am your shield and your very great reward." With this understanding, what did God give Abraham under the stars?
_____
_____

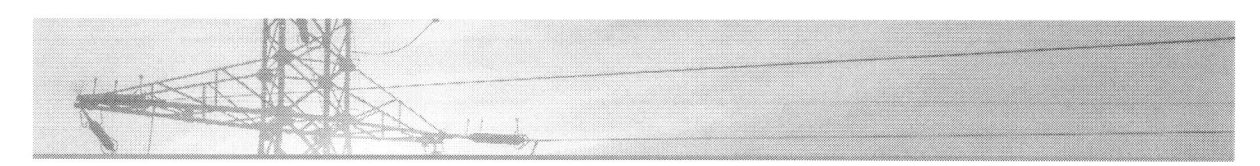

The God of the universe, who spoke all things into existence, offers Himself to a disheartened nomad who had to start counting stars to gain the perspective needed to remember both God's promise and the fact that He was with him. God offers Himself to us, too. He is always interested in a deepening relationship with us, first and foremost.
So what is my response? I can choose to develop **Practice #1 - Preparing Myself** by laying down distraction, disappointment and disinterest, and refocus on Him.

As one of the on-call chaplains at our nearby hospital, we're taught tools of being "present" when we are ministering to patients. These basic tools are somewhat intuitive, and perhaps you have been trained in similar "tools": good listening skills, posture, eye contact, appropriate questions. I believe there are similar "tools" for us the spiritual sense of being "present" also. You'll notice these tools of being present with people are all action oriented. How I listen, how I observe and pay attention, how I ask questions and interact, all require sensitive effort and action on my part.

Take a moment and write out what actions you can take to personally prepare yourself to be present (awake, alert and attentive) with the Lord:

_____

_____

_____

_____

Practice #2 - Repositioning Myself
Have you ever sat on the couch or somewhere so long that your foot or entire leg goes to "sleep"? You need to reposition yourself to get the blood flowing again. The numbness from sitting in one position and cutting off circulation to a particular part of our body is obviously not good for us. The numbness of spiritual inactivity isn't good for us either. It's a wise practice to reposition ourselves. The good news is that we can move to re-establish good circulation physically and spiritually.

Take another look at Luke 11:9-12 (previous page). Circle the words "ask," "seek," and "knock" in that passage. In the Greek, these words are present tense with the active voice and imperative mood. Greek has these distinctions, which affect our understanding of the meaning. When we put all this together it means that we are the ones initiating this action and it is a continuous action, rather like a lifestyle. And this isn't a suggestion, it's a command. We are to continuously ask, seek, and knock.

How do you think asking, seeking and knocking could possibly be helpful to "reposition" ourselves to be present in His presence?

_____

_____

Some of us may be wondering what it looks like to "ask, seek and knock". There are no set formulas for this. It is a choice to be awake, alert, attentive and active. But some suggestions include the following:

1) Daily reading of scripture
2) Journaling and recording progress, questions, requests
3) Practicing conversation with God - both asking and listening (prayer)
4) Studies of scripture (you are in one now!)
5) Time and energy spent with others who are asking, seeking and knocking
6) Evaluating your schedule and laying aside activities of one sort to make time for spending energy on study, listening, exercising of Spiritual gifts, and sharing

There are other ways to "ask, seek and knock," but these are some suggestions to get going. This practice of "repositioning" ourselves will help keep us from experiencing the "numbness" of poor spiritual circulation. We do the asking, seeking and knocking; Jesus does not do this for us. He is speaking of a lifestyle of initiating action and effort to know, find, and discover - to be "present". When we accept the responsibility to increase our "spiritual circulation" by initiating and putting effort into our experience of His presence, we have repositioned ourselves for a deeper experience with God in His presence.

For those who like very practical suggested activities, especially if you are struggling out of the tent of disappointment, I suggest writing out Isaiah 41:10 on an index card or something that will last awhile and put it where you will see it every day. Repeat it out loud at least once a day (shut the door; no one will mind): **"So do not fear, for I am with you; do not be dismayed, for I am your God. I will strengthen you and help you; I will uphold you with my righteous right hand."**

What do we do when we have earnestly asked, sought and knocked, but nothing seems to happen? What do we do with our disappointments and dismay and the apparent lack of "good gifts" from our Heavenly Father? Beloved of God, don't give up. Start "counting stars" as Abraham did: bring every disappointment and disheartening situation to Him and make an offering of it all at His feet, and keep choosing to believe. This would be a very practical and powerful act of worship. And then choose to keep practicing being prepared and practicing repositioning yourself by asking, seeking and knocking, but perhaps refocusing on the Person of God, not your requests. He is with you. He loves you. He sees you and He knows you.

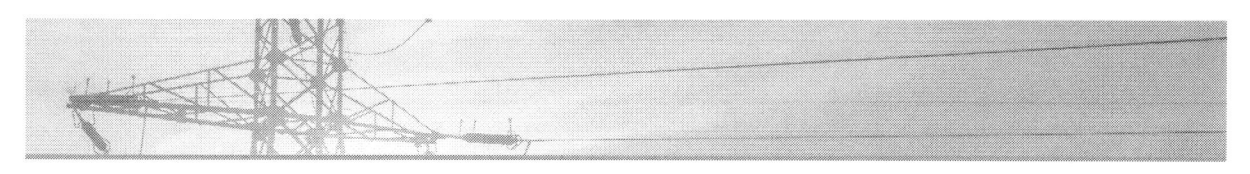

During a time of grief with many questions about why things happen as they do, I was most certainly asking, searching and knocking. I couldn't seem to get any satisfactory answers. But then one day as I simply and honestly opened my heart once again to Him, I believe I heard, "I'm not withholding the answers you seek. I long to share them with you. But the answers you seek would not make sense to you on earth. It would be like "smelling the color nine" (referencing a popular song at the time - "Smell the Color 9" by Chris Rice ©2000.) The words would be there, but it would not make sense. Trust me that I love you, I understand, and someday we will take a walk along the shores of heaven and I will share it all with you."

Some argue that the "activities" of heaven will not include walks with Jesus. That's ok - we don't have to agree about that. The point is that I have chosen to entrust my ultimate questions to His ultimate answers in heaven someday. In the meantime, I have found my peace with these particular questions in the enveloping character and presence of God, believing in Him and growing in my trust in His character and goodness. And so I ask, seek and knock about other things while I walk this earth with Him now.

So what are you asking for? Think carefully about this...your Good Heavenly Father is listening to your heart. Write down your thoughts in the form of a prayer here:

_____
_____
_____
_____

What are you seeking? What do you want to find? Write down your thoughts in the form of a prayer here:

_____
_____

Can you name a door that you would like to have opened for you or to you? Put your thoughts in the form of a prayer here:

_____
_____
_____
_____

Are you willing to keep knocking until it opens (or He redirects you)? _____

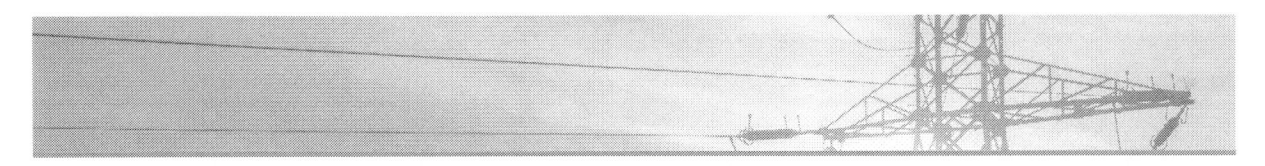

Are you willing to share these answers with a friend or small group and pray over them together? _____

It may be that you stared at this page and nothing came to mind. That's ok; it's a journey. Perhaps you could ask God to bring something to your mind, while you take initiative and put efforts into being present with Him, one day at a time.

On day 101 under the power lines I heard: "My presence is the atmosphere, the oxygen to your spirit. It's always about relationship: My person to your person, My heart to your heart. After all, I made you in My image so we can relate together, partner together and be one family together. There is no power apart from relationship with Me - just effort and human activity, often delusion and often, most often, disappointing. But in Me there is everything you need. Walk with Me, beloved, step by step, each moment remembering My presence and purposes, and I will guide you, help you, teach you, empower you. Oh that you would know my dreams for you! That would energize your soul, fill your mind, encourage your heart. We will walk together, beloved, in the paths and purposes I've chosen, and My power will be active in, upon and through you - for the Kingdom, and your soul will be thrilled."

A prayer as we close

Thank you, Father. I choose to remember that You are present with me so I can be present with You. I ask for Your help, Your kind prompting and reminders. I choose to prepare myself, laying down my distractions and disappointments at Your feet. I choose to reposition myself by asking, seeking and knocking, interacting with You as we go. I choose to march on in the purposes for me that You have chosen. In the powerful name of Jesus, amen.

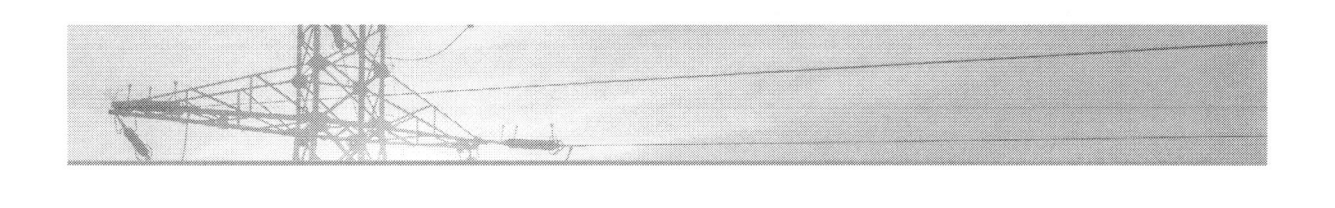

Chapter Eight

The Power of Walking in Agreement

I've been fascinated with history for some time. The story of how we have navigated through the ages is interesting to me. Recently my attention was drawn to one of the greatest agreements ever made to change our modern world. It may surprise you to know that what has been called the Louisiana Purchase is considered just such an agreement.

The Kingdom of France controlled the Louisiana territory from 1699 until it was ceded to Spain in 1762. In 1800, Napoleon hoped to re-establish an empire in North America and regained ownership of Louisiana. The dream of a new empire failed, and Napoleon decided to sell Louisiana (territory) to the United States. We originally sought to purchase only the port city of New Orleans and its adjacent coastal lands, but quickly accepted the bargain. The Louisiana Purchase occurred in 1803, just 27 years after the difficult birth of our nation, during the term of the third President of the United States, Thomas Jefferson. Before the purchase was finalized, the decision faced Federalist Party opposition; they argued that it was unconstitutional to acquire any territory. Jefferson agreed that the U.S. Constitution did not contain explicit provisions for acquiring territory, but he did have full treaty power and that was enough. So we gained 828,000 square miles, which included land from fifteen present U.S. states and two Canadian provinces (which we obviously negotiated to Canada later). This nearly doubled the size of our nation for $15 million, which was about three cents per acre at the time. It's known as one of the best land "deals" of modern times. (Wikipedia)

My attention was drawn to this well-known agreement because it was something of a surprise to the Americans involved in its negotiations. They were prepared to spend $10 million just for New Orleans and its coastal lands, so this deal was considerably larger than they anticipated.

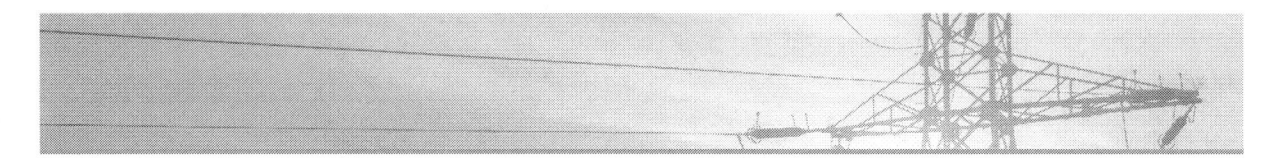

Those who now live in the United States have all been impacted by this agreement. I was born and raised in Minnesota in a region west of the Mississippi. According to the boundaries of the bargain, if the deal had not gone through I may have grown up speaking French. Bon dieu!

Some agreements have long-range effects - generational effects in fact, impacting the entire world. Our nation didn't just grow in size; it grew in influence, and eventually in power. With all our flaws and issues, we are still known as the most powerful nation on earth, God help us.

As I considered this recently, I was drawn back to the moment of the Louisiana Purchase and imagined their surprise as the Americans heard the amount of land they could acquire in the deal.

I believe in our study today we may find ourselves surprised at the largeness of the "deal" God is wanting to make with us to partner together for vast spiritual territorial gain for the Kingdom.

On Day 44 under the power lines I heard, "As I move and work, you'll need to keep seeking My face to keep connected and protected. The flesh is easily distracted and lured away by "good things". As you seek My face, continuing in intimacy and deliberate disciplines to stay focused, I will continue to empower you by My Spirit. If you continually seek My face, what I begin I will continue to its completion. When I say a thing, when I plan something, I look for those of My people who will agree with me no matter what, and will walk the necessary path. Is this in your heart?" We'll explore this "necessary path" of agreement today.

A suggested prayer to begin

Lord, I ask for wisdom and understanding today, the ability to grasp and know what it is You are saying in Your word. Thank You for being with me and teaching me all that You have to show me today. In Jesus' name, amen.

On day 97 under the power lines I heard, "Only those who will walk with Me are entrusted to be vessels of My power to a powerless world. The degree that we walk together is the degree to which you will be entrusted to wield My grace-filled, love-encompassing, life-transforming power. Walk with Me, Beloved. I choose to walk with you and enable you to bring My power to the powerless. Will you walk with Me? No preconceived notions, no hard-earned opinions, no agenda other than Mine, no carelessness or apathy. I will bring the life-giving energy to walk with Me so that I can entrust to you My intentions to free others. Walk with Me, Beloved. No turning back."

Write out Amos 3:3:

_____

_____

_____

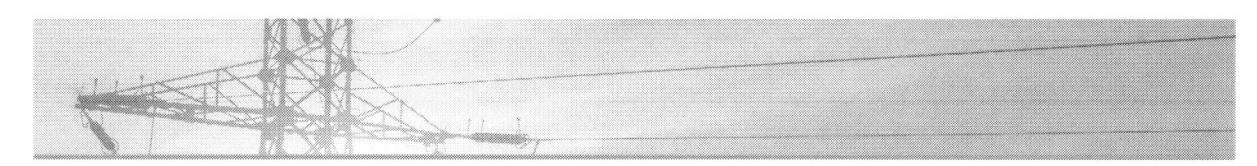

Walking with God in agreement is very similar to walking with someone on a path. You have to have some agreement on walking together or you will veer off and go separate directions.

So how do we "walk with God" in agreement? First, let's see what how we used to walk before we began our relationship with Christ:

Ephesians 2:1-3: "And you were dead in your trespasses and sins, in which you formerly **walked** according to the course of this world, according to the prince of the power of the air, of the spirit that is now working in the sons of disobedience. Among them we too all formerly lived in the lusts of our flesh, indulging the desires of the flesh and of the mind, and were by nature children of wrath, even as the rest."

According to verse 1 above, why were we walking "according to the course of this world...indulging the desires of the flesh and of the mind...by nature children of wrath"?

_____

Perhaps this is why in recent years we've seen so many science fiction movies and television shows that highlight those who are dead but are still walking around. There seems to be an unfortunate parallel to this scripture. But there's good news, and it's not science fiction. Verses 4-9 remind us of the change that has come in our "walking" because of Jesus:

"But God, being rich in mercy, because of His great love with which He loved us, even when we were dead in our transgressions, made us alive together with Christ (by grace you have been saved), and raised us up with Him, and seated us with Him in the heavenly places in Christ Jesus, so that in the ages to come He might show the surpassing riches of His grace in kindness toward us in Christ Jesus. For by grace you have been saved through faith; and that not of yourselves, it is the gift of God; not as a result of works, so that no one may boast. For we are His workmanship, created in Christ Jesus for good works, which God prepared beforehand so that we would **walk** in them."

We're alive now in every way because of God's great mercy and love, and the grace in Jesus Christ by which we have been saved! And because of this, what are we now "walking in"?

_____

Who prepared these beforehand?

_____

The Greek word "walk" in this Ephesians 2 passage (*peripateo*) is interesting, being formed from two words: *peri*, meaning "around" or "near" and *pateo*, meaning putting your foot down as in treading upon a path. The use of *peripateo* in this passage denotes "either the state in which one is living, or the virtue or vice to which they are given." Before being "made alive" together with Christ, we walked in our sins and trespasses, deadened to the life and power of God. But now God has "raised us up" with Christ, and "seated us with Him" so now He might "show the surpassing riches of His grace and kindness towards us in Christ Jesus."

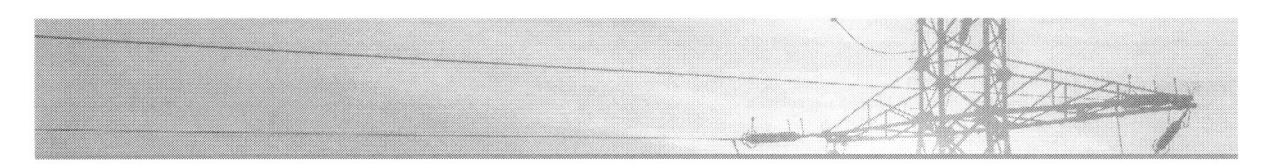

His grace and kindness includes being His workmanship, created for good works in Christ, so we will walk in them. You don't have to create these good works; they are already created for you, created long ago with you in mind. We walk these out with Him as we go.

Colossians 2:6-7 says, "Therefore as you have received Christ Jesus the Lord, so **walk** in Him, having been firmly rooted and now being built up in Him and established in your faith, just as you were instructed, and overflowing with gratitude."

Circle the word "received". This Greek word means to take to oneself, join to oneself. When we chose to receive Jesus, we chose to be joined with Him. So the word "as" in this passage tells us that in the same way, in like manner, we are to walk with Him: Joined together! I take my steps along the path joined with Christ, and He will reveal the "good works" created for me as we go.

How do I stay "joined" with Christ as I walk? On day 52 under the power lines I heard, "My eyes search to and fro for those who seek My face, whose hearts are set on pilgrimage, so we can travel the path of My plans together. My power enables these ones to keep walking when others fall."

Being joined with Christ on the paths we walk once again has to do with my heart being "set on pilgrimage" with Him. Pilgrimage is simply walking the way, or path. Verse 5 of Psalm 84 (NIV) speaks of this pilgrimage; but the psalm is so good, I've printed the entire psalm here:

[1] How lovely is your dwelling place,
   Lord Almighty!
[2] My soul yearns, even faints,
   for the courts of the Lord;
   my heart and my flesh cry out
   for the living God.
[3] Even the sparrow has found a home,
   and the swallow a nest for herself,
   where she may have her young—
   a place near your altar,
   Lord Almighty, my King and my God.
[4] Blessed are those who dwell in your house;
   they are ever praising you.
[5] Blessed are those whose strength is in you,

    whose hearts are set on pilgrimage.
⁶ As they pass through the Valley of Baka,
   they make it a place of springs;
   the autumn rains also cover it with pools.
⁷ They go from strength to strength,
   till each appears before God in Zion.
⁸ Hear my prayer, Lord God Almighty;
   listen to me, God of Jacob.
⁹ Look on our shield, O God;
   look with favor on your anointed one.
¹⁰ Better is one day in your courts
   than a thousand elsewhere;
   I would rather be a doorkeeper in the house of my God
   than dwell in the tents of the wicked.
¹¹ For the Lord God is a sun and shield;
   the Lord bestows favor and honor;
   no good thing does he withhold
   from those whose walk is blameless.
¹² Lord Almighty,
   blessed is the one who trusts in you.

According to verse 7 above, what happens to the pilgrim whose heart is set on the path?

_____

I "set my heart," choosing to keep walking joined with Him, and He strengthens me to keep walking. What a partnership!

All partnerships have agreements in order for the partnership to keep functioning as needed. Each partner brings something to the partnership. One of the words in scripture used to describe this is the word "covenant". God has made several covenant agreements with mankind. I'll list these chronologically.

1 - In Genesis 9:8-17, God makes a covenant agreement with **Noah**. Describe that agreement here:
_____.

What does God ask Noah to do in this covenant agreement? _____

What a partnership! God always seems to do the heavy lifting in agreements with mankind.

2 - In Genesis 12:1-3, God makes **Abraham** a promise to bless him. But it isn't until Genesis 15 that the actual ceremony (common in those days) took place. God promises him

many descendants (remember the stars?) and land in order to fulfill the promise of blessing, not only to Abraham but through him. According to Matthew 1, who is the ultimate descendant of Abraham?

___

Oh, what a partnership! Again God did the heavy lifting in this covenant agreement. So many, many "stars" because of Jesus. I am one, and if you have been "joined with Christ," so are you.

3 - The book of Exodus describes a covenant God made with **Moses**, called the **Mosaic** Covenant. This is for the nation of Israel, and Jeremiah 31:31-34 tells us a new covenant is coming instead: "Behold, the days are coming, says the Lord, when I will make a new covenant with the house of Israel and with the house of Judah -- not according to the covenant that I made with their fathers in the day that I took them by the hand to lead them out of the land of Egypt, My covenant which they broke, though I was a husband to them, says the Lord. But this is the covenant that I will make with the house of Israel after those days, says the Lord: I will put My law in their minds, and write it on their hearts; and I will be their God, and they shall be My people".

Oh, what a partnership! Some say this has been partially fulfilled as we who are not of the nation of Israel (Gentiles) have been grafted in and included in the New Covenant of Jesus Christ (See Hebrews 8). Whatever your beliefs are about the fulfillment of this particular agreement with Moses, it's clear God once again does the heavy lifting: putting the law in their minds, writing it on their hearts, being their God. It's interesting that nothing is listed in Jeremiah 31:31-34 for them to do, but they are to be:

___.

4 - In 2 Samuel 7:12-13, God makes an agreement with **David**. What did God promise to do?

___.

It's interesting that there is nothing that God tells David he must do in this agreement, but God does tell him that he is not to do something (that David planned to do). What is that?

___.

How long will David's kingdom last?

___

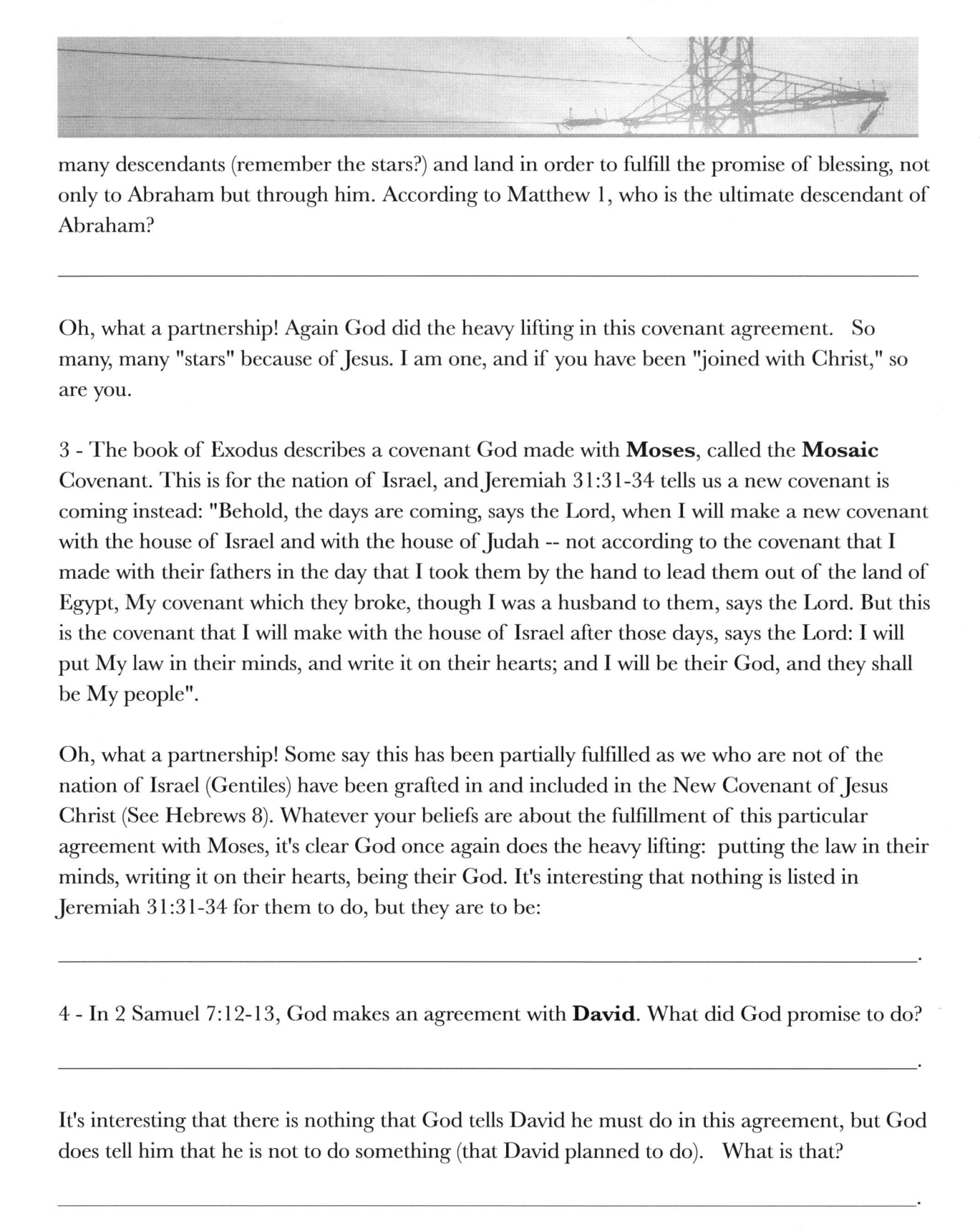

Looking once again at Matthew 1, Jesus is the "son of ___ and the son of Abraham."

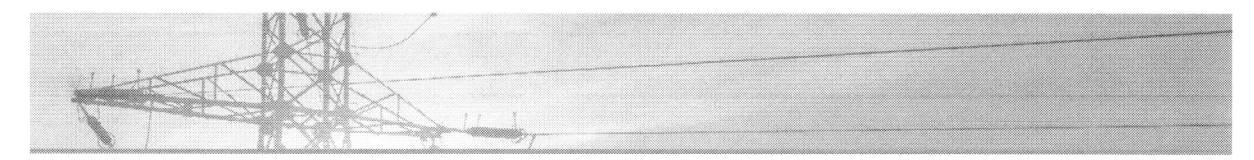

God promises that the Kingdom will continue eternally, and that is accomplished through David's lineage through Jesus Christ. David simply obeys and doesn't do something, and God does everything. What a partnership!

5 - **The New Covenant** is first mentioned by Jesus Christ at what we call the "last supper," described in Luke 22:20: "In the same way, after the supper He took the cup, saying, 'This cup is the new covenant in My blood, which is poured out for you.'"

Hebrews 8 goes into more detail about Jesus being the "mediator" of this New Covenant - an agreement far superior to any other agreement on earth. In this new covenant, this new agreement, we give Him all of our sin and brokenness in repentance and He gives us His righteousness! This is far better than the Louisiana Purchase! Far better than all we can think or imagine. God saves us through relationship with Jesus Christ, gives us empowering grace to walk in agreement with Him, lights our path with His very presence, and guides us in loving care as we go. He does all the heavy lifting. What a partnership! (More loud expressions of gratitude would be appropriate here - shut the door, no one will mind. Or write it out in the margin.)

I Corinthians 1:9 says, "God is faithful, through whom you were called into fellowship with His Son, Jesus Christ our Lord." The word "fellowship" is the Greek word "*koinoia*", which is from a word meaning a "partner, associate, comrade, companion". In this partnership, I partner with Jesus by continuing to agree with Him as we walk together. As I do this, I'll also find myself with others who are joined with Christ, agreeing with Him as we all walk with Him. The fellowship grows.

But here's the "rub," as they say: Our partnership is not about me, or the benefits to me, but about the Kingdom. If we are truly partners with Jesus as I Corinthians 1:9 says, then we will be doing what Jesus would do, caring about what Jesus cares about, working in Kingdom ways. This is practical and tangible as we "walk" with Him each day. If our partnership with Jesus is simply theoretical, we've missed the boat.

So here are some practical ways in which agreeing with God as one of His partners would work:

1 - When you read scripture, tell God you agree with Him or ask Him to make it clear to you so you can agree with Him. For instance, using Ephesians 2:10, I would tell God that I agree I am His workmanship, created in Jesus for the good works He has prepared for me. I agree that I will walk in these good works as He reveals them to me as I go. If this is also something that you agree to do, write out your agreement in your own words here:

_____

_____

How would you agree with God about Titus 2:11-14? Write out your agreement (or questions for God) in the space below:

_____

_____

_____

_____

2 - When you pray, ask God to show you how to partner with Him throughout the day. If something comes to mind, write it down and determine to do it. If you are willing to do this, write out your agreement here:

_____

_____

_____

_____

3 - When we walk in agreement with God, we will find ourselves side-by-side with likeminded believers who are also walking in agreement God. We can partner together in Kingdom work and activities. Ask God to show you likeminded fellow believers who are walking with Him in agreement. Write down someone who may have come to mind and set up a time to have a conversation. _____

As we continue to walk with God, encountering Him each day, we learn to walk with His heart, His power, His love flowing in and through us as our "new normal".

On day 88 under the power lines I heard, "You cannot learn of or experience My power without consistent, holy encounters with Me. As you seek Me and learn of Me, My power is released in its natural way (to Me). Become accustomed and adjusted to My 'normal'. Power is flowing."

A suggested prayer as we close

Father, thank you for the amazing invitation to partner with You to walk with You in agreement each day. I want to know how to do this more and more. And so I will continue to seek You, learn of You, and make my choices to walk closely, listening and paying attention. I know I can do this with Your help and guidance, Your presence and power. In Jesus' name, amen.

Chapter Nine

Power to Walk with Purpose

I went to the Oregon coast with a friend over a weekend to "work". My friend is a talented artist, and we both decided one day that we would take the time to get away and focus: She would paint and I would write this study. Truly this lovely beach home was to be a retreat from the noise and clatter of life, so there was no internet service; but I had been using online study tools, so after breakfast one morning I told my painting friend to have a good day and went off to find a coffee shop or somewhere that had an internet connection. My GPS system told me where the nearest coffee shop was located, but I could also find other places to sit and study; so I asked the Holy Spirit to guide me. Sometimes locations matter, sometimes not so much, but it's wise to check in. I had a clear thought that the cafe was the place, with some Kingdom purposes, so I ordered some healthy food and settled in with their delicious coffee.

A little while into my study time, I noticed a delightful 2-year-old boy and his mother walking by me to the restroom. In that moment I believe I heard the Lord speaking to me about this charming child. I wrote down the words I heard, words of encouragement and kindness from God's heart to this child and his family. When the mom and boy returned to their table, I got up and brought the paper I had written and gave it to them with the simple words of, "I know this is a bit unusual, but I believe this is for you." And I sat down at my table once again and sipped my coffee.

Over the years I've learned to pay close attention and take the risk of doing such things, agreeing to fulfill the "assignments" that come in the middle of a day or task, sometimes simply and sometimes profoundly.

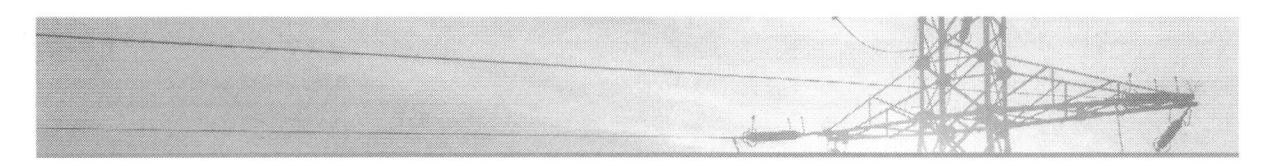

On day 33 under the power lines I heard the Lord say, "As you walk in the assignments I give you, My power is free to flow through you to others, bringing transforming love, life and light to them and their situation. When My people walk in their assignments, listening, following, breathing My word, they will find themselves aligning to Me and others; they will find themselves marching side by side with likeminded, one-heart people doing the same. As they do this, they are strengthened and ready. And the whole region will be changed, for My purposes, for the Kingdom."

I'm not saying this one little encouraging piece of paper changed the whole region for the Kingdom, but it did bring smiles and appreciation from the family. One member came to my table later to specifically tell me that it encouraged them. Although I fulfilled my assignment when I simply obeyed and gave them the paper, it was kind of God to let me see how it encouraged them.

How did I find the gumption to get up out of my comfortable chair and focused task to risk handing someone an encouraging word, someone I didn't know? I'm learning to walk in the assignments He gives, through His grace and power.

Write out John 14:12 here:

_____
_____
_____
_____

To understand these "greater works", we'll need the spirit of wisdom and revelation mentioned in Ephesians 1:17. We'll unpack this today, exploring how to cooperate with the Lord in our daily lives, fulfilling Kingdom assignments in the power of God.

A suggested prayer as we begin

Lord God, I open my heart and mind to You today. Teach me how to walk in any assignment You give me. Reveal what I need to know and understand. I ask for the spirit of wisdom and revelation so my eyes will see and I will know the hope and power of Your calling me to partner with You. I pray this with an expectant heart in Jesus' name. Amen.

On Day 95 I heard, "My power is always flowing, always working. But big displays and small manifestations are the same from My hand. The only thing different is My purpose in and through it. My heart never changes - it always beats with love for you. My mind never stops thinking of you and My plans for you. My hands never stop working on your behalf to further the Kingdom! But my feet! Oh, My feet are your feet - will you connect...by cooperating with all I intend? It's only one step at a time, but you must move your feet. You could put them on top of mine, you know...and we'll dance the steps of the redeemed. Others will see and want to join."

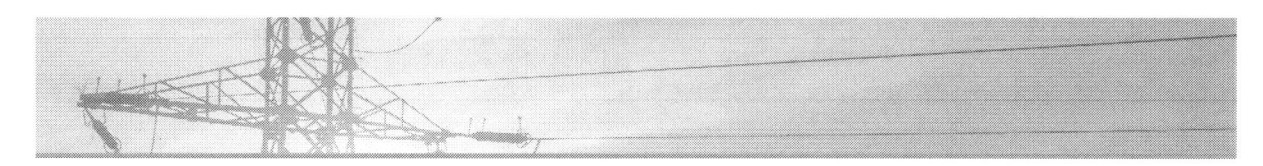

Little children will sometimes put their feet on top of their daddy's feet so they can dance together. We can learn the steps that way. I believe God referenced that to me under the power lines so I could remember that we can learn to take steps, but these steps are to be with Him, not for Him.

God never intended that our "service" just be deeds and actions aimed at pleasing Him. I know that sounds sacrilegious. We saw in our study last week that He intends that we partner and walk in agreement with Him, not do things for Him. He is looking for listening partners, willing hearts and lives to walk with Him and His intentions, not fearful servants trying to somehow appease a demanding God, somehow learn a difficult "dance" and somehow please a disapproving father. Please hear me: He is not mad at you. He is not angry, and - some may find this one hard to believe - He is not disappointed in you.

It's impossible for Him to be disappointed in you as His child, because when He looks at you He sees the completed work of Jesus within you, through the Spirit. He sees a victorious and fulfilled person. And when God speaks to you, He always speaks from this complete perspective into your moment. That is why the angel called Gideon (who was minding his own business, trying to thresh some wheat in a converted wine press) a "valiant warrior" (Judges 6:11-24). I can imagine Gideon said, "Who, me?" When God speaks to you, it will always seem a bit beyond your present level of growth because He sees the completed you, the "you" on assignment walking in the power of God.

Matthew 5:48 says, "Therefore you are to be perfect, as your heavenly Father is perfect." The Greek word "perfect" here is "teleo" - fulfilling the purpose for which it was created. He always has your purposes for which you were created in His mind when He thinks of you.

When we do things we know (or discover) are not Kingdom ways, He brings the correction and counsel to make a better decision, but never with disappointment - only with love and purpose. In fact, it's always a clue to who is trying to influence you by the way in which the correction and counsel is coming to you. God's way will be clear and corrective, but always with an encouragement to go a better/healthier direction. It is not incriminating, critical or condemning. He will call a matter truthfully, but it is always paired with a loving call to walk with Him on a better path. He chooses to use His kindness as a way to lead you to repentance (Romans 2:4), a change of mind that leads to a change of direction and action. If you hear condemnation, critical thoughts (or words) or discouragement about who you are, rather than clarity about what you did, I highly recommend you put those thoughts aside and ask God to bring His words to you in His way (and crank up the worship music; that seems to help).

I like how The Message translates Romans 8:1-2: "With the arrival of Jesus, the Messiah, that fateful dilemma is resolved. Those who enter into Christ's being-here-for-us no longer have to live under a continuous, low-lying black cloud. A new power is in operation. The Spirit of life in Christ, like a strong wind, has magnificently cleared the air, freeing you from a fated lifetime of brutal tyranny at the hands of sin and death."

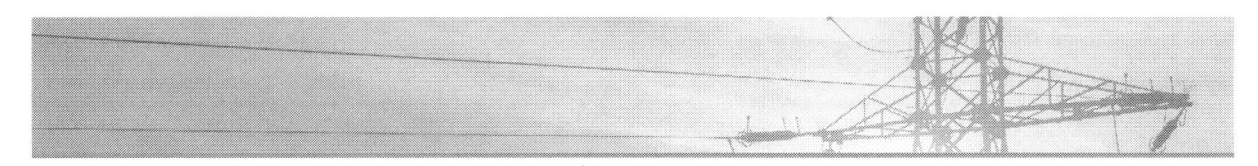

Why does He see you as a completed person walking in the "cleared air" of the Spirit as a partner and fulfilling your assignments with Him? Because when you receive Jesus and His gift of a restored life, you have received the Holy Spirit who brings everything you need for life and godliness.

Write out 2 Peter 1:3 (NIV):

_____

_____

_____

_____

There's our word *dynamis* again, which we are coming to understand as the intentional divine influence upon my heart and resource to bring whatever is needed according to the purposes of God.

Take another look at the verse. Does it say His divine power will (future) give us everything we need, or does it say it has given (past tense) everything we need? I agree with you: It says "His divine power has given everything we need for a godly life." It's already done. The clue to understanding this is in the last half of the verse. Note how Peter says that God's divine power has given us everything we need for a godly life through...

_____

_____

The word "through" here means "the ground or reason by which something is or is not done." Since God says it's done, let's study the ground or reason for it in this verse.

The word "knowledge" does not mean data points or what is often called "head knowledge". It's the Greek word "*epignosis*", which finds its root in a similar word meaning "to know thoroughly, accurately, well." *Epignosis* has the meaning of a person actively involved in knowing something or someone so well and accurately that they recognize and perceive a thing to be what it really is.

You probably have heard the story of how they train people in catching counterfeit dollar bills. I found an interesting blog by Tim Challies, who wanted to find out for himself if what others have been saying is true: that "Federal agents don't learn to spot counterfeit money by studying the counterfeits. They study genuine bills until they master the look of the real thing. Then when they see the bogus money they recognize it." So he ventured to a nearby

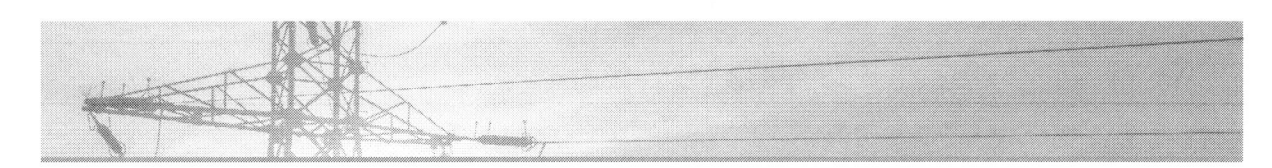

Canadian bank (where he lives) and asked if he could talk to someone about this. His full story can be found here: http://www.challies.com/articles/counterfeit-detection-part-1. He was told that agents are taught to distinguish a genuine bill with the phrase, "touch, tilt, look through, look at."

The first step is to touch the bill. Currency is printed on unique cotton-based paper; a false bill will often feel false. Counterfeits tend to feel "waxy," and there are other tactile clues.

Having touched the bill, the agent's next step is to "tilt" the bill. There is a holographic image on each bill that shows all the colors of the rainbow, as well as other clues that will appear when it's tilted and studied.

The third step is to look through the bill, holding it up to the light and noticing several identifying features: watermarks and other specific indicators.

Then finally the step of "look at": looking closely at the fine-line printing and other features that are so fine they can't be adequately reproduced by the casual counterfeiter.

Mr. Challies says he was taught these basics and then given a shot at seeing if he could do it himself with a stack of bills. Here is what happened according to his blog: "I soon learned that identifying counterfeit currency is not a terribly difficult task. When a person knows what to look for, when he has been trained to examine the bill for particular identifying characteristics, identifying genuine from fraudulent can be done with great accuracy, even on the basis of only a small amount of training..."

No matter how long we have walked with the Lord, we can continue to "touch, tilt, look through and look at" our Jesus. We can grow in our knowledge (*epignosis*) of Him each and every day. And when we do this, our intimate and accurate knowledge of Him causes us to partner with Him so we can walk in His power and purposes, on assignment, spotting counterfeits a mile away.

On day 54 under the power lines I heard, "To really know My power, you have to experience it. My heart longs for people to know My power, so that the lies about Me can be broken and they will see who I really am - all they need in My heart of love for them. Don't let the demands of your life keep you from the fullness of My love and power. I am right here". He is right here.

Write what you see happening or explained in these verses below, and what it might encourage you to do today. I've used the "touch, tilt, look through and look at" system to help us focus. Perhaps we could stretch our thinking in these ways, considering how we could "touch" Jesus, considering how we could move to change our perspective somehow ("tilt"), considering how to look through Jesus' eyes ("look through") to understand His heart, considering how to look at Jesus Himself.

Touch - Luke 8:43-48:

How I might "touch" Jesus today:

Tilt - Luke 15:3-10:

How I might "tilt," or change my perspective of Jesus today:

Look through - Matthew 11:28-30:

How I might see what Jesus sees today:

Look at - John 1:14, Philippians 2:6-11:

_____
_____

How I might get a better view of Jesus today:

_____
_____
_____
_____

It is through our ever-increasing knowledge of Jesus that we increasingly experience the *dynamis* of God within us to live godly and effective lives. We can walk each day "on assignment" with purpose as He guides and leads us. **Whether it's a cafe on the coast or a cubicle in the office, a marketplace boardroom or grocery market, a classroom or living room, a nursery or noon meeting, a phone call or conversation, He has given us what we need to partner effectively as we listen and live the adventure of walking with Him, one moment at a time.**

On day 53 under the power lines I pondered the still-bright half moon in the early morning sky. I heard, "I placed the stars, called them by name. I breathe life. I create. I cast down non-life. I lift up My beloved, My creation - the people I carry in My heart....all of you. If I can place planets, keep them spinning, am I able to place you in the right place, keep you walking? My power brings life. Speak life today."

What life-giving words do you see in the verses above (or other verses) that you could share with someone today? Write them down, have them ready:

_____
_____
_____
_____
_____
_____
_____

Will you pray and ask the Lord to show you when and how and to whom you can share these life-giving words?

_____

_____

_____

_____

We saw in our first lessons that God's love is always in action. What other love-action is God asking you to agree to do? Is there an assignment that comes to mind as you consider this in His presence in prayer? If so, write it out here:

_____

_____

_____

_____

God loves to confirm and affirm within the community of His people, His family. Share what you have written with someone, or your small group, and pray over it together.

Yes, I have shared and prayed with others for confirmation: _____

It is up to me to choose to live "on assignment," bringing my effort and energy to bear into each moment to listen and walk with Him as He guides me. My agreement with Him as I walk with Him is a vital part of our partnership, and the key to effective ministry for all of us who call Him Lord and Savior. The adventure of living this life of agreement and purpose is unparalleled, and I believe He anticipates with us the joy of walking it out together.

On day 31 under the power lines I heard, "Every day I provide opportunities for My people to be conduits of my transforming power. Each expression and manifestation is unique, but My power is constant. One moment leads to another. Stay, learn, and move as I direct. It will spill over, run down, change lives, grow the Kingdom...all in close relationship and communication with Me."

A suggested prayer as we close

Lord God, today I choose to walk with You and to be on assignment as You direct me. Today I choose to be alert and live well, listening and doing whatever is before me according to the purposes You have for my life. I will do my work well, I will love my family and others well, I will listen and partner with You and others well, all with Your strong influence, Your power in my heart. I choose to agree with You and become a trusted partner today with Your help. In Jesus' name, amen.

Chapter Ten
Power to Be Powerful

I debated about the title of this last chapter for some time. It's a dangerous title in some ways, but I decided that's appropriate. I've come to understand that one of the reasons God asked me to meet Him under the power lines, and subsequently write this study, is to correct some incorrect thinking on my part. I confess to you that I believe I thought of God's power as something to be utilized, brought down on earth in some way.

On day 21 under the power lines I heard, "Yielded vessels are like lightning rods, drawing power to the earth from a charged atmosphere to specific location. I look for yielded vessels." That seemed to reinforce the idea of unpredictability and dangerous power. But of course when you add that one piece of information to the other 100 pieces of information God shared under the power lines, it provides a broader understanding - and I hope your concept of the power of God has been broadening and clarifying as we go.

It took me a while to realize that I also thought that if we knew the "code," we could somehow wield the power of God (picture a Star Wars light saber here). I know that at times I hoped it could happen that way. God knew this was in my mind and heart, and has graciously been helping me gain insight and a better understanding.

My granddaughter, Harper, is just about 3 years old. When she wants to "unlock" my phone (yes, I have some adorable and fun games on my phone for my granddaughters), she grabs my finger and starts to push buttons, hoping I'll get the idea. Her vocabulary is large for 3 years old (and rather constant), but it's so much easier to just grab my hand.

Perhaps if we're honest we'll admit our desire to "grab God's hand" and unlock whatever code there is to wielding His power in circumstances or situations that have come our way. I believe He understands that. I believe He knows it's hard for us to feel so powerless at times - times when we're standing by the hospital bedside of a loved one, or when we hear of yet another tragic shooting or catastrophe or disaster or heartache. We simply want to grab His hand and unlock the code and unleash His power to "fix it". I believe He understands. I've also come to believe He wants to "fix it" far more than we ever would.

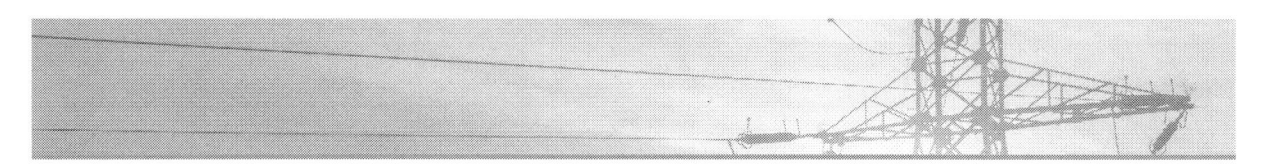

As we consider this tendency of ours, and the concept of being powerful today, let's begin with prayer.

A suggested prayer

Lord God, thank you for understanding me, understanding my sense of helplessness at times. Thank you for helping me as I study today. I'm opening my heart and mind to You, in Jesus' name. Amen.

Context is always vital when studying the Bible. It's too easy to just grab a verse and run with it, making it mean whatever you'd like it to mean. So I believe we need to set the context of understanding the power to be powerful by understanding God's heart a bit better today.

I've found a great website (https://achristian.wordpress.com/2006/12/06/the-father-heart-of-god/) that listed some verses that show His passion and heart for His beloved (all of us). It's written from The Message translation in the form of a letter from God's heart to yours, and I highly recommend we take the time to absorb these statements. I also highly recommend you speak this out loud (shut the door; no one will mind).

"My Child…

You may not know Me, but I know everything about you - Psalms 139:1-6
I know when you sit down and when you rise up - Psalms 139:1-6
I am familiar with all your ways - Psalms 139:1-6
Even the very hairs on your head are numbered - Matt 10:29-31
For you were made in My image - Genesis 1:27
In Me you live and move and have your being - Acts 17:28
For you are My offspring - Acts 17:28

I knew you even before you were conceived - Jeremiah 1:4-5
I chose you when I planned creation - Ephesians 1:11-12
You were not a mistake, for all your days are written in My book - Psalms 139:15-16
I determined the exact time of your birth and where you would live - Acts 17:26
You are fearfully and wonderfully made - Psalms 139:14
I knit you together in your mother's womb - Psalms 139:13
And brought you forth on the day you were born - Psalms 71:6

I have been misrepresented by those who don't know me - John 8:41-44
I am not distant and angry, but am the complete expression of love - 1 John 4:16
And it is my desire to lavish My love on you - 1 John 3:1

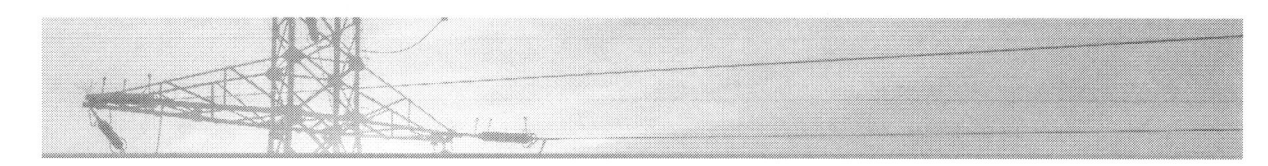

Simply because you are My child and I am your Father - 1 John 3:1
I offer you more than your earthly father ever could - Matthew 7:11
For I am the perfect father - Matthew 5:48
Every good gift that you receive comes from My hand - James 1:17
For I am your provider and I meet all your needs - Matthew 6:31-33

My plan for your future has always been filled with hope - Jeremiah 29:11
Because I love you with an everlasting love - Jeremiah 31:3
My thoughts toward you are countless as the sand on the seashore - Psalms 139:17-18
And I rejoice over you with singing - Zephaniah 3:17
I will never stop doing good to you - Jeremiah 32:40
For you are My treasured possession - Exodus 19:5

I desire to establish you with all My heart and all My soul - Jeremiah 32:41
And I want to show you great and marvelous things - Jeremiah 33:3
If you seek Me with all your heart, you will find Me - Deuteronomy 4:29
Delight in Me and I will give you the desires of your heart - Psalms 37:4
For it is I who gave you those desires - Philippians 2:13
I am able to do more for you than you could possibly imagine - Ephesians 3:20

For I am your greatest encourager - 2 Thessalonians 2:16-17
I am also the Father who comforts you in all your troubles - 2 Corinthians 1:3-4
When you are brokenhearted, I am close to you - Psalms 34:18
As a shepherd carries a lamb, I have carried you close to My heart - Isaiah 40:11
One day I will wipe away every tear from your eyes - Revelation 21:3-4
And I'll take away all the pain you have suffered on this earth - Revelation 21:3-4
I am your Father, and I love you even as I love My son, Jesus - John 17:23

For in Jesus, My love for you is revealed - John 17:26
He is the exact representation of My being - Hebrews 1:3
He came to demonstrate that I am for you, not against you - Romans 8:31
And to tell you that I am not counting your sins - 2 Corinthians 5:18-19
Jesus died so that you and I could be reconciled - 2 Corinthians 5:18-19
His death was the ultimate expression of My love for you - 1 John 4:10
I gave up everything I loved that I might gain your love - Romans 8:31-32
If you receive the gift of My son Jesus, you receive Me - 1 John 2:23
And nothing will ever separate you from My love again - Romans 8:38-39

Come home and I'll throw the biggest party heaven has ever seen - Luke 15:7
I have always been Father, and will always be Father - Ephesians 3:14-15
My question is…Will you be My child? - John 1:12-13
I am waiting for you - Luke 15:11-32

Love, Your Dad, Almighty God"
Selah.

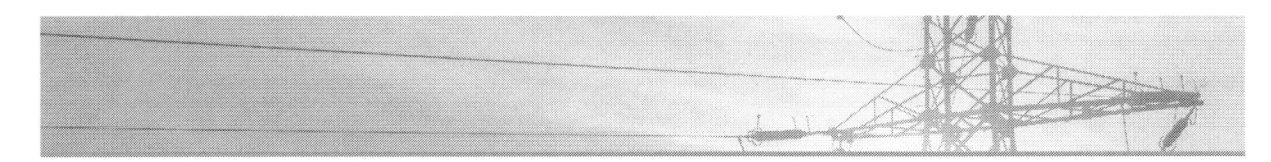

If there was something that was stated above that was hard to grasp or agree with, look up the verse listed and consider a deeper study into that particular topic. Don't take our word for it; check it out yourself like the Bereans (Acts 17:11). Talk to some friends who are also studying His words and scriptures, who can give you some insight and help.

Today we'll take a deeper look at the statement "I'm able to do more for you than you can imagine", from Ephesians 3:20. I've printed Ephesians 3:14:-21 here:

> [14] For this reason I bow my knees before the Father, [15] from whom every family in heaven and on earth derives its name, [16] that He would grant you, according to the riches of His glory, to be strengthened with power through His Spirit in the inner man, [17] so that Christ may dwell in your hearts through faith; and that you, being rooted and grounded in love, [18] may be able to comprehend with all the saints what is the breadth and length and height and depth, [19] and to know the love of Christ which surpasses knowledge, that you may be filled up to all the fullness of God. [20] Now to Him who is able to do far more abundantly beyond all that we ask or think, according to the power that works within us, [21] to Him be the glory in the church and in Christ Jesus to all generations forever and ever. Amen.

How does God want to strengthen us? (Verse 16) _____

through _____ in the inner man.

Why does He want to strengthen us? (Verse 17) "so that _____

_____

What does He want us to comprehend? (Verse 18)

_____

_____

_____

Why does He want us to comprehend and know the love of Christ? (Verse 19)

_____

_____

_____

_____

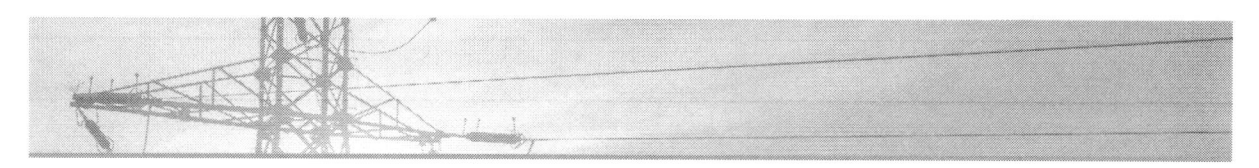

The Greek word used for "know" in verse 19 is *ginōskō*, which is used here to mean, "to learn to know, come to know, get a knowledge of, perceive, feel, to become known." According to this verse, we come to know the love of Christ more and more and, as we do, we are "filled with the fullness" of God. The Greek word used for "fullness" is "*plērōma*", used here to mean "filled with the presence, power, agency, riches of God...".

In other words, apparently we cannot be filled with the presence and power and resources of God without the experience and growing personal knowledge of the love of God in Jesus Christ. This is why we began this Bible study series with the lesson "Power to Be Loved and to Love". We are circling back to this basic, foundational truth: **To be truly powerful, filled with the presence and power of God Almighty, I must be filled with His love.** Then I will see people as God sees them and He can entrust His gifts and ministry to me.

Shawn Bolz has written a book entitled Translating God that puts it this way: "*When Jesus was moved by compassion, it was not just a feeling he had, but an understanding and conviction of what those people meant to the Father. Their value in the eternal realm was not just based on their immediate healing; Jesus could see what would happen if they had a connection again to God, if they could walk in the fullness of the purposes they were created for. He also saw them as though they were already eternal, and he pulled them into that place just by loving them. Ultimately, he laid down his life to reconnect them to the Father because he believed in the value of that connection.*" (Chapter One, pages 20-21).

It is surprising to me that people name Jesus as their Savior and Lord but then go about with literal hatred for others on this poor planet - especially those who do wrong and terrible things. They seem to feel justified to get angry on God's behalf.

We need to help each other remember that God is working, and He is the judge of all mankind. Our job is to see the value in others that God sees and call it out in love and kindness. Confrontation will be necessary at times, but God opens the way with love, not angry judgment. **Remember, God's love is not sentimental fuzziness, but clear and compassionate actions that bring people to Himself.** I have been a poor conduit of His love at times, but am committed to grow in my understanding and experience of His love. I want to be an effective disciple bringing people to Jesus, so they will walk in the fullness of the purposes God has for them.

We've seen in our previous lessons that God is seeking partners on earth who will do His will "on earth as it is in Heaven" - those who will agree with God and do what He asks. I believe the power to do mighty things through the Holy Spirit must flow through a humble, loving heart. Otherwise we are noisy gongs and clanging symbols, producing nothing of lasting value - even those things such as speaking all knowledge and prophecies and sacrifices (I Corinthians 13).

Looking back at our Ephesians 3 passage, review once again what God is able to do (verse 20):
_____
_____

And review once again where this power, the "*dynamis*" of God is working (verse 20):
_____
_____

There is a qualifying word between those two phrases: the word "**according**" - "Now to Him who is able to do far more abundantly beyond all that we ask or think, according to the power that works within us...". This is the Greek word "*kata*", a preposition. According to Thayer's Greek Lexicon, its usage denotes "motion or diffusion or direction from the higher to the lower..."

Reviewing again, where does this power come from? _____
(Sometimes it's good to simply write something out more than once.)

What is the outcome of this "*dynamis*" of God working within us (verse 21)? _____
_____
_____

It has always helped me to think of God's glory as His "revealed excellence". It can be seen, it is revealed, and it is excellent. We honor Him and reveal His excellence when we choose to cooperate with the power of God working within us, doing far more than we could ever imagine! Clearly the glory and honor belongs to God as we experience His love and operate as powerfully loving people wherever He sends us, wherever we go.

On day 28 under the power lines I heard, "What you do with My power dictates how it will manifest in the future. Mistakes are covered with grace, but pride/arrogance will cut it off and it will require great humility, repentance and My mercy for it to flow again. Be very careful. The regulator is love. If you hunger for My power but do not have My heart - My deep, abiding love - I cannot trust you and I will withhold. Watch for those who love. I will entrust much to them in these days."

We are never more powerful than when we choose to love - choosing actions that draw people to God. Compassion is the compass, empowered by the Spirit, endowed with gifts to be deployed to strengthen, encourage and bless. What an adventure! More loud expressions of gratitude would be appropriate here (shut the door; no one will mind), or write it out in the margin.

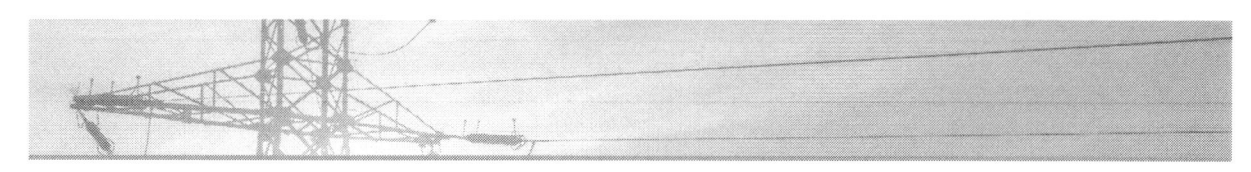

On day 51 under the power lines I heard, "My power is always available, every moment, to the child of Mine that loves, moves in compassion and understands My authority. Wisdom is yours, My child, to know and live this....if you will choose it."

Will you choose to be a powerful person? If this is your desire, ask God to increase your capacity to receive and live out His love. Write out your prayer here:

_____

_____

_____

_____

Are you willing to be given any gift He chooses to encourage and bless others? (See list of spiritual gifts in 1 Corinthians 12:8-10, Ephesians 4:7-13 and Romans 12). If so, write out your agreement with God in the form of a prayer here:

_____

_____

_____

_____

_____

On day 58 under the power lines I heard, "My word brings focus, clarity and stability when learning of My power. It must go hand in hand with each experience of My presence and power. Study, absorb, learn, and ask for wisdom and revelation. These days are too important for you not to know and understand."

God bless you, beloved child of God, as you journey along with Him, growing in knowledge and understanding. He loves you and is with you; you can trust Him.

On day 42 under the power lines I heard, "As I work, be ready to move and work in love and purity of heart. My power may best be seen and felt in quietness and trust. Trust me. There is grace in these days as you learn and grow..."

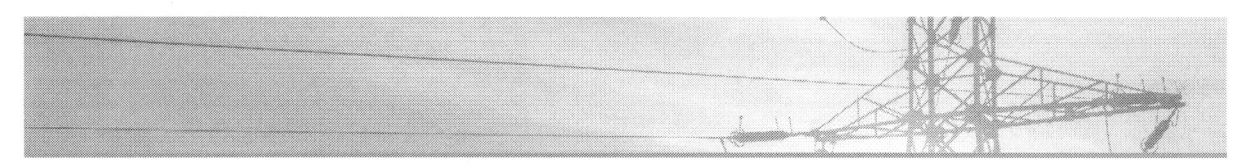

A suggested prayer as we close

Thank you, Lord Jesus, for Your enabling grace. I believe You are trustworthy and I choose to trust You in this journey. Thank you for teaching me and guiding me. I choose to walk with You each day, learning as I go, experiencing Your presence and power and love, and fulfilling the assignments You give me to love others. I know that with You, all things are possible! In Jesus' name, amen.

Conclusion

I hope this study in the Power of God has been helpful to you. I hope as we have walked together "Under the Power Lines" that you have been able to consider, study and grow in your journey with Jesus, the One who loves you so. No matter what is ahead, I believe great things are in store for those who will focus, listen and walk with Jesus as He directs. We can fulfill the beautiful "job description" Jesus gave us from Isaiah 61, which He quoted in Luke 4 when in the temple. Although Jesus quoted only the first few verses, I've printed the whole encouraging passage here:

> [1] The Spirit of the Lord God is upon me,
> Because the Lord has anointed me
> To bring good news to the afflicted;
> He has sent me to bind up the brokenhearted,
> To proclaim liberty to captives
> And freedom to prisoners;
> [2] To proclaim the favorable year of the Lord
> And the day of vengeance of our God;
> To comfort all who mourn,
> [3] To grant those who mourn in Zion,
> Giving them a garland instead of ashes,
> The oil of gladness instead of mourning,
> The mantle of praise instead of a spirit of fainting.
> So they will be called oaks of righteousness,
> The planting of the Lord, that He may be glorified.
> [4] Then they will rebuild the ancient ruins,
> They will raise up the former devastations;
> And they will repair the ruined cities,
> The desolations of many generations.
> [5] Strangers will stand and pasture your flocks,
> And foreigners will be your farmers and your vinedressers.
> [6] But you will be called the priests of the Lord;
> You will be spoken of as ministers of our God.
> You will eat the wealth of nations,
> And in their riches you will boast.
> [7] Instead of your shame you will have a double portion,
> And instead of humiliation they will shout for joy over their portion.

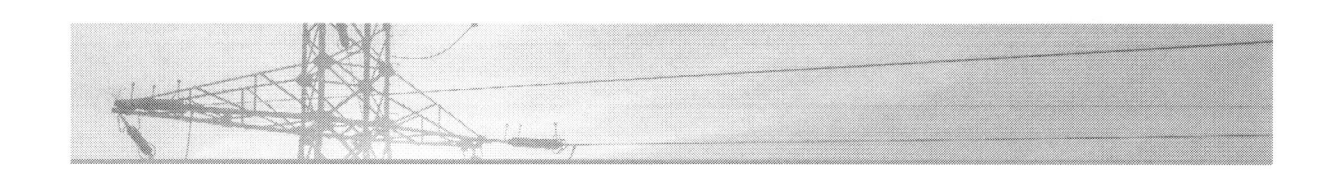

Therefore they will possess a double portion in their land,
Everlasting joy will be theirs.
[8] For I, the Lord, love justice,
I hate robbery in the burnt offering;
And I will faithfully give them their recompense
And make an everlasting covenant with them.
[9] Then their offspring will be known among the nations,
And their descendants in the midst of the peoples.
All who see them will recognize them
Because they are the offspring whom the Lord has blessed.
[10] I will rejoice greatly in the Lord,
My soul will exult in my God;
For He has clothed me with garments of salvation,
He has wrapped me with a robe of righteousness,
As a bridegroom decks himself with a garland,
And as a bride adorns herself with her jewels.
[11] For as the earth brings forth its sprouts,
And as a garden causes the things sown in it to spring up,
So the Lord God will cause righteousness and praise
To spring up before all the nations.

Selah.

On day 43 under the power lines I heard: "The time is coming when I will move in ways you have not seen before, ways that will amaze you, as I pour out My love and power for transformation
.....for you, your family
.....My family
.....your city
.....your county
.....your state
.....your nation and beyond."
This deeply moves me to keep going! I hope you will also.

I told the Lord on Day 100 under the power lines, "Here I am, Lord!" and believe I heard Him say, "My power comes unexpectedly, arising from who I AM - I AM and always have been, always will be. It is not conjured up, deserved or coerced. I cannot be conjured up, deserved or coerced. I always work, and always do so from My heart and purposes for My Beloved....all of you. It cannot be understood by human effort, only by human willingness to experience who I AM. I AM other. I AM here. I AM totally loving you every minute of your day, working in power you may not see but certainly can discern if you will train your spiritual senses in this. I will help you. I want you to see and know Me. I always have, I always will." Amen!

With Gratitude

I'm so grateful for the team of people who joined together for this "Under the Power Lines" Bible study project - people who proofread, formatted, illustrated, prayed and encouraged. Thank you Nancy Dodson, Phyllis Gates, Lucinda Brown, Jessica Broich, Steve Hardgrove, Judy Carson, Lee Patten, the Northside Community Church Wednesday morning womens' Bible study group, so many others, and of course Jim, my beloved husband.

If you would like to contact me, please do so at endicottdiana@yahoo.com.

Made in the USA
San Bernardino, CA
17 March 2017